New Covenant Life

THE POWER OF NEW TESTAMENT LIVING...
DAY BY DAY

NEIL SILVERBERG

New Covenant Life
The Power of New Testament Living
Day by day

MASTER
PRESS

ISBN 978-0-9993750-3-7

For information:
MASTER PRESS
3405 ISLAND BAY WAY, KNOXVILLE, TN 37931
Mail to: publishing@ masterpressbooks.com

CONTENTS

INTRODUCTION

Ask many Christians today what the New Covenant is, and they are likely to point you to the second half of the Holy Bible. Some would not even be able to do that since few are aware the term *testament* is simply another word for covenant. Not being able to verbalize the term '*New Testament*', my Jewish father referred to each part of the Bible as the '*front of the book*' (Old Testament) and the '*back of the book*' (New Testament). I once read the fifty-third chapter of Isaiah at a family Passover and my father stopped me midstream, reminding me that he had prohibited me from reading from the back of the book. Imagine his surprise when I told him I was reading from Isaiah, one of his own prophets (from the *front of the book*).

Perhaps we can dismiss my father's ignorance since he wasn't a believer. But sadly, just as my father didn't know the difference between the front of the book and the back of the book, few believers today know the difference between the Old Covenant and the New Covenant. You'd think this would be the most fundamental thing all believers should know, but it isn't. This general ignorance in knowing the New Covenant shows up, not only in our biblical ignorance, but also in the quality of our Christian lives. It is not unusual today for believers to carry around a low-grade guilt over what they consider to be their poor performance when it comes to living the Christian life. One of my responsibilities in a church where I served as a teaching pastor was to pray with people at the end of each service. Asking each one what they requested prayer for, many would confess to feeling condemned and not knowing how to deal with it. Not having time to give them a sufficient answer, I told them to make an appointment to come and talk with me in the coming week. I would often end up with a full slate of counseling appointments for the coming week, which were really teaching sessions where I taught justifying grace as a New Covenant reality. Though many of these people had been in the Church for years, they were strangers to the riches of grace revealed in the New Covenant.

We should not be surprised at the level of ignorance when it comes to an understanding of the New Covenant in the Church today. Much of what passes for preaching and teaching more closely resembles that of the Old Testament prophets than the New Testament apostles with its denunciations for failing to obey. Few are ever taken to New Covenant mercies which alone has the power to change lives. In the first church I was part of, we had a service on Tuesday nights I humorously referred to later as *Condemnation Night.* That was the night you found out how miserably you had failed that week at living the Christian life. When the message was over, we all rushed to the front of the church to ask forgiveness and recommit ourselves to try harder in the upcoming week. Needless to say, we were back the following week, licking our wounds and pledging once again to do better.

This lack of grounding people in New Covenant reality can also be seen when it comes to our attempts at discipling those who are new in the faith. Looking through many discipleship courses offered in most churches today, we can only conclude once a person is converted, all that is needed is to teach them how to perform. Rare indeed is that discipleship course which places emphasis on rooting and grounding believers in the grace of the New Covenant rather than resorting to behavior modification. This is especially the case when it comes to young people who have grown up in the Church. Despite years of church attendance and being raised in Christian homes, many remain strangers to the Gospel. In a high school Introduction to the New Testament class I was teaching in our church, I asked the students the simple question, "What is the Gospel?" A student immediately blurted out, "It's instructions on how to live." I spent most of the rest of the class attempting to teach them how that was a perfect description of the Law rather than the New Covenant.

Thankfully, there is a renewed emphasis on the Gospel in the Church. Gospel books, conferences, and discipleship courses are common fare in much of the Church. We must remember though, at the heart of the Gospel, is the New Covenant itself. We must make sure that our churches fully learn and embrace all that the New Covenant is. Browsing a website recently, I found the following statement: "Without the New Covenant, there is no Gospel message, no Christianity, no salvation, no inclusion of the Gentiles in Gods promises. Without the New Covenant, the Jews would still be bound by the Old Covenant having to make animal sacrifices for the covering of their sins, and we, as Gentiles, would remain on a fast track to hell!"[1]

As we shall see in this book, the New Covenant is not a written document. I don't mean to deny the fact the second half of our Bible contains twenty-seven books called the *'New Testament.'* Nor am I suggesting studying the New Testament so as to live out its truth is not vital to Christianity. What I do mean is the New Covenant is not a set of rules one must follow but a *new* way of approaching God. Failing to be properly instructed in the New Covenant, we may default to living under the Old, even while claiming to be New Covenant believers. In fact, if we're not careful, we can easily turn

---

1 www.indefenceofthegospel.com/content/new-covenant

the New Testament itself into a rule book where Jesus is viewed primarily as a 'Second Moses' who came to give us a shot in the arm and tell us to try harder. Over the years, I have argued with believers who defended a certain mode of baptism based on the New Testament and killed all those who disagreed.

This is a book about the glory, the grandeur, the majestic New Covenant which God made with his people. The New Covenant is *New* precisely because it is a thoroughly different way of approaching God than was ever known. It's not merely a jazzed up version of the Old. The writer of Hebrews quotes from the amazing prophecy of Jeremiah where God promises to make a New Covenant with Israel (Hebrews 8:8-12). In the verse which precedes it, he tells them why there was a need for a New Covenant— *"For if that first covenant had been faultless, there would have been no occasion to look for a second"* (8:7). The Old Covenant, though given by God, was not without fault, and therefore had to be replaced. It was not faulty as a revelation from God, but simply due to the fact that it was based on promises that were conditioned upon the Israelites' perfect obedience. And the simple fact remains, the Israelites *"did not continue in my covenant"* (8:9). As we shall see, they could not keep it because of the weakness and sinfulness of the flesh.

So, at a certain moment in time, God sent his Son to issue a covenant totally different from the old. Simply stated, it did not depend on human performance at all! God instituted a covenant whereby he took human obedience out of the equation. It would not be *"like* the covenant that I made with their fathers on the day when I took them by the hand to bring them out of the land of Egypt"* (Hebrews 8:9, italics mine). That first covenant was based on how well the Israelites obeyed and kept his commandments. Since the New was not *like* the Old, it could only mean the Covenant was not dependent on what human beings did but solely on what God did.

That is why there simply is nothing like the New Covenant, nor has there ever been in the realm of religion. All religions share in common the simple fact they require human performance. Not so when it comes to the New Covenant; it is totally focused on what God did through the perfect work of his Son, Christ Jesus.

This book is loosely arranged around an examination of the main features of Jeremiah's great prophecy of the New Covenant (31:31-34), but it is not limited to that. Many other Scripture references are examined as well, but Jeremiah's amazing words comprise the main substance of the chapters. As such, it is both *theological* and *pastoral*. It is theological because it is based on a revelation of God first given in the Old Testament and then expounded in the New. New Testament books like Romans and Hebrews exhaust the language while describing the length, breadth, depth, and height of New Covenant theology.

I write not merely as a theologian, but as a pastor as well. My heart aches deeply to see whole groups of God's people living as strangers to the New Covenant; they often view Jesus as little more than a life-coach, giving advice on how to live a better life, instead of the great Inaugurator of a powerful new way of approaching God. It pains me to no end to see God's elect trying to live New Covenant values under an Old Covenant basis. I long to see people set free to live all that the New Covenant promises.

I feel somewhat qualified to write this book not only because of my acquaintance as a Jew with the Old Covenant and over forty years of studying the New, but also due to my own struggle to live the Christian life under an Old Covenant mindset. Even though at eighteen years old God powerfully saved me and brought me into the Church through the new birth, it was many years before I learned what the New Covenant really was. My early church experience was essentially a Christianized version of the Old Covenant, replete with laws, statutes, and fearful warnings. We could relate well to the writer of Hebrews' characterization of those who heard the audible voice of

God: "whose words made the hearers beg that no further messages be spoken to them" (Hebrews 12:19). It seems the only time we referred to the New Covenant was at our communion services when we cited Jesus' words at the Seder, "*This cup is the new covenant in my blood*" (Luke 22:). I remember how strange those words sounded against the backdrop of our normal diet of fear and dread. Indeed, it was at such communion services that my desire to learn what those archaic words *New Covenant* meant was first formed.

Though this is a theological treatment of the subject, I wrote it for the man in the street who still thinks Christianity is a glorified attempt at keeping the Old Covenant (though he probably doesn't know it). I am burdened deeply all who claim his name burst into the glorious freedom of the New Covenant. May God take these feeble words and use them to bring a new generation into the freedom of New Covenant living. Amen.

CHAPTER ONE

UNDERSTANDING
THE OLD COVENANT

I once heard the story (don't know if it is true) of a young Scottish girl who was stopped on her way to a Reformation meeting at a time when attending them was illegal. Asked by the authorities where she was going, she knew she couldn't lie. So, after a slight pause, she said, *"My brother has died, and I am on my way to a family meeting to hear the reading of the will."* With that, the authorities let her go.

Besides being the best description of a New Testament church meeting I ever heard, this young girl knew something that often escapes many believers: That the two sections of our Bible we call Old, and New *Testaments* are really two *covenants* God has entered with his people throughout time. As the young Scottish girl stated so clearly, the New Testament is a *will* (so is the Old Testament). And if they are wills, that means there had to be the death of the testator for these wills to be in effect. The *Old* Covenant was ratified by the death of innocent animal victims as prescribed by the Law. But the basis of the *New* Covenant rests on better promises and required a better sacrifice

(Hebrews 8:6). Nothing less than the death of God's own Son would put that covenant into effect.

While there are other covenants mentioned in the Bible, these two form the major divisions of our Bible, each a record of God working in human history to form a people for himself. The first five books of the Old Testament known as *Torah* (instruction or law) contain a history of Israel's beginnings, the covenant which God gave them on Mt. Sinai, and the laws and regulations contained in it. Similarly, the first five books of the New Testament are also historical, setting forth the life, ministry, death, resurrection, and ascension of the Son of God (Gospels), as well as the first thirty years of the advance of the Gospel in the earth (Acts). Both Testaments, therefore, start with five historical books explaining how these covenants were initiated by God in their corresponding histories.

There is another way to view each of these Testaments, what is often called the *spiritual* way. *They represent two, differing ways to approach God and have a relationship with Him.* The *Old* Covenant approach is that of *works*, meaning a person was required to obey the Law in order to receive its blessings. It is summed up well by the statement of God to Moses: *"If a person does them, he shall live by them"* (Leviticus 18:5). In other words, a person receives life as a result of their obedience to all the commandments of the Law. The Rabbis counted and concluded there were 613 commandments in the Law. So, a person's standing with God was determined by his diligence to perform all of these commandments.

The *Old* Covenant is not only first when it comes to the structure of our Bibles, it is the covenant we naturally gravitate to as sinners. We are automatically wired to make our *works* (what we must do in order to be right with God) the basis of our approach. Why? Because as sinners blinded by sin's power, we mistakenly believe we can please God by something we do. All religions essentially share this approach, whether Judaism with its works—

righteousness obtained through Torah observance, or Islam, with its Quran regulating how one should dress, talk, worship and behave. Their operating principle is, "*I obey; therefore, I am accepted.*" All human religions, therefore, are *'works'*-based.

But at a given moment in history, God sent his Son into the world to introduce a new way of approaching God (although foreseen in the Old Testament). It was totally unlike the Old Covenant of works which preceded it. The world had never seen a religion such as the Gospel of grace where God reconciles men and women who trust in the work of *Another.* Because human beings are utterly powerless to do anything about their condition, the good news of the Gospel presented the One, Jesus Christ. He made it possible for sinners to live under a *New* Covenant with true forgiveness of sins and power to break free from sin's dominion.

COVENANT IS ABOUT RELATIONSHIP

To understand what the New Covenant is and how it functions, it is essential we first understand some basic aspects of the nature of biblical covenants. The central idea of covenant is that God seeks relationship with human beings he has made in his image and likeness. Whether it's divine covenants between God and man or human covenants between fellow human beings, relationship is the core component of covenant.

We get some idea of what covenant is by comparing it with human *agreements* or contracts. We are all familiar with such agreements where each party pledges to do certain things according to the contractual terms of the agreement. When I bought my house, I had to have a certain measure of trust in my realtor, due to the fact I didn't read all of the fine print of my mortgage contract. For all I know, I might have been contracting to mow my realtor's lawn for the rest of her life! But I did make sure the basic facts were understood: what I was paying for the house and what that meant in terms of monthly payments. I am now bound to the terms of this contract, and it has a definite effect on the way I live (as evidenced by the fact each month I write a mortgage check).

Similarly, biblical covenants between people mirror human agreements and contracts with some differences. Walter Elwell demonstrates the similarity when he defines covenant as "a compact or agreement between two parties binding them mutually to undertakings on each other's behalf."[2]

There is a great difference though between human covenants and divine covenants. Divine covenants between God and human beings are always initiated by God Himself. Again, Walter Elwell describes the theological idea behind covenant:

> *Theologically (used of relations between God and man) it denotes a gracious, undertaking entered into by God for the benefit and blessing of man, and specifically of those men who by faith receive the promises and commit themselves to the obligations which this undertaking involves.*[3]

As we read the Bible, we discover that God has taken the initiative to enter relationship with human beings through the instrument of covenant. Covenant is the *means* by which he relates to us. Without God initiating these various covenants, we would have no chance of entering relationship with God. And God initiated two great covenants throughout human history, both of which were "gracious undertakings" for the "benefit and blessing of man:" the *Old* Covenant, inaugurated at Mount Sinai through the mediation

---

2 *Evangelical Dictionary of Theology*, Walter Elwell, page 276
3 ibid: pg. 276

of Moses under which the nation of Israel was constituted the people of God, and the *New* Covenant, mediated by the Son of God by which the new people of God, the Church, has been brought into being.

A CONDITIONAL COVENANT

The online dictionary Wikipedia defines covenants in this way: Some covenants are *conditional* (if one party does A, then the other party will do B), just as with a present-day contract. But generally, ancient covenants are *unconditional* (each party commits to a certain action, regardless of whether the other party keeps the covenant).

The Old Covenant has been described as both *conditional* and *unconditional*. It was *unconditional* in that God *alone* took the initiative to enter into covenant with Israel, vanquished Egypt with ten plagues and brought his people out of Egyptian bondage. That God sovereignly initiated his plan is evident by the fact his choice of them had nothing to do with any supposed virtue they possessed, but in order to fulfill the promise made to the fathers (Deuteronomy 7:6-8). Israel was God's people on the basis of *grace* alone. Yet even though they were his by grace, the fulfillment of his promises was based on their willingness to *obey* his voice (Exodus 19:5-6). That is what is meant by the *conditional* aspect of that covenant. If they obeyed, they would receive the things promised, but if they didn't, he would reject them as his people. That Israel understood this is evident by the fact that, after Moses rehearsed all the words of the covenant to them, the people answered, "all the words that the Lord has spoken we will do" (Exodus 24:3).

This idea of *conditional* covenant is easy for us to grasp. When we were young, our parents made promises to us based on our having met certain conditions. A father, for example, may promise his daughter a new car if she finishes high school with a certain grade-point average, but it is up to her as to whether she will receive it. She must first meet the *conditions* if the promise is to be fulfilled. In the same way, God made promises to Israel under the Old Covenant, conditioned upon the people's obedience (Deuteronomy 28). He promised blessings in their families, blessings in the fields, blessings in their livestock, and blessings in every way if they perfectly keep the Law of God:

> *"And if you faithfully obey the voice of the Lord your God, being careful to do all his commandments that I command you today, the Lord your God will set you high above all the nations of the earth. And all these blessings shall come upon you and overtake you, if you obey the voice of the Lord your God."*

> *Deuteronomy 28:1*

What if they refused to obey the covenant? Just as the promises of blessings were so wonderful if they obeyed, so horrific were the curses that would fall upon them if they chose to be disobedient (see Deuteronomy 28:15- 68). God would essentially treat them as his enemies and would curse them in their physical bodies, cause crop failure, and defeat in battle against their enemies. In a word, they would be the object of every curse for their disobedience just as they would receive every blessing if they obeyed.

No Conditions
(JEREMIAH 31:32)

As we will see in the next chapter, Israel was doomed to condemnation since they could not keep the Law. Paul sums it up nicely when he says, "The law brings wrath, but where there is no law there is no transgression"

(Romans 4:15). Wherever the Law appears, the result is wrath since fallen human beings can't keep it. God must judge sinful human beings for their failure to keep the Law. That is what is meant by the statement, "The Law brings wrath."

This wrath did not rest on Israel alone, but Gentiles as well are under the wrath of God for failing to keep the Law, even though they did not possess the written Law. In Romans 1:18-2:16, Paul demonstrates how Gentiles, while not having written Law, demonstrated they had the Law written into their consciences so that they also are without excuse. Even a non-Jew who has never read the written Law feels guilt when he or she violates it. I have talked to people who described how they experienced guilt the first time they lied, committed adultery, or stole.

Since both those who have the written Law and those who don't stand condemned, what hope is there? There is only one hope, and that is the bringing in of a *better* covenant: "But as it is, Christ has obtained a ministry that is as much more excellent than the old as the covenant he mediates is *better* since it is enacted on better promises" (Hebrews 8:6).

What does the writer of Hebrews mean when he calls the New Covenant a "*better* covenant?" He answers that in the last clause of Hebrews 8:6: "... it is enacted on *better* promises." What made the New Covenant promises better than those given in the Old? The answer is found in a phrase which appears in the great prophecy of the New Covenant given by the prophet Jeremiah, which the writer of Hebrews goes on to quote. In Hebrews 8:9, he describes the New Covenant as being: "*not like the covenant that I made with their fathers.*" This covenant was totally different than the previous covenant he had made with their fathers, which was the Old Covenant.

How would it be different? Since the Old Covenant was a *conditional* covenant, this covenant would be unconditional. In other words, *it would not be a covenant of works in which God's blessings depended on what one did.*

Rather, it would be a different kind of covenant altogether in which God promised to do certain things regardless of what men and women do. In other words, promises were given *without* conditions.

In fact, when you go to look for the conditions, you find that there aren't any: *The conditions of the old have become the promises of the new!* The New Covenant, therefore, is the covenant of grace announcing what God would do for those who receive it.

Why, then, did he give the Old Covenant first? As we shall see in the next chapter, the Old Covenant was given as a means of preparing us to receive the New Covenant. It is only when the Old Covenant does its work of deeply convicting us of sin and bringing us under judgment as transgressors that we will ever be persuaded of our need for a New Covenant. More about this in the next chapter.

CHAPTER TWO

THE BROKEN COVENANT

I t is one of the most memorable stories in the entire Old Testament. After bringing his people out of Egypt through mighty deliverances, Moses, directed by God, led them to Mount Sinai where they were to be adopted as the chosen people of God. Moses was summoned to the top of the mount to hear this loving invitation of the Creator to make Israel his own:

Thus you shall say to the house of Jacob, and tell the people of Israel: You yourselves have seen what I did to the Egyptians, and how I bore you on eagles' wings and brought you to myself. Now, therefore, if you will indeed obey my voice and keep my covenant, you shall be my treasured possession among all peoples, for all the earth is mine; and you shall be to me a kingdom of priests and a holy nation. These are the words that you shall speak to the people of Israel.

Exodus 19:3-6

After that, Moses was instructed to prepare Israel for her encounter with God. The people were given three days to purify themselves in readiness to hear their great God's voice. On the third day, the entire mountain was engulfed in thunders, lightnings, and a thick cloud, followed by the sound of a trumpet and God's voice beckoning Moses to come up the mountain and speak with God. The entire mountain quaked so that even Moses himself trembled in fear (Hebrews 12:21). It was then that God spoke to two million people (600,000 men not including women and children) his *ten words.* So powerful was this moment that Moses, looking back forty years later, reminded Israel of their unique privilege:

> *For ask now of the days that are past, which were before you, since the day that God created man on the earth, and ask from one end of heaven to the other, whether such a great thing as this has ever happened or was ever heard of. Did any people ever hear the voice of a god speaking out of the midst of the fire, as you have heard, and still live? Or has any god ever attempted to go and take a nation for himself from the midst of another nation, by trials, by signs, by wonders, and by war, by a mighty hand and an outstretched arm, and by great deeds of terror, all of which the Lord your God did for you in Egypt before your eyes? To you it was shown, that you might know that the Lord is God; there is no other besides him. Out of heaven, he let you hear his voice, that he might discipline you.*
>
> *Deuteronomy 4:32-36*

Moses remained on the mount forty days and nights, receiving the Law with its commandments as well as the regulations for worship in the

Tabernacle (Exodus 21-31). This included the two tablets containing the Ten Commandments which were written by the finger of God Himself (Exodus 32:16). No people were ever as privileged as Israel to hear the voice of the living God and live, and to receive tablets written by the finger of God himself.

Sadly, while Moses delayed on the mount, Israel grew tired and impatient and bated Aaron into making and worshipping a golden calf as a token of God. When Moses came down and saw the people unrestrained, worshipping this false god, his anger burned against the people and he *"threw the tablets out of his hands and broke them at the foot of the mountain"* (Exodus 32:19). This symbolized not only Israel's failure in the matter of the golden calf, but as a prophetic statement that the Old Covenant was a *broken* covenant.

ISRAEL'S FAILURE

One powerful example that the Old Covenant is a broken covenant is Moses himself, the mediator of the covenant. Though God used him in the capacity of mediator, he failed to enter into the land of promise because he himself did not keep the covenant (Numbers 20:12). This is in spite of the fact that up till that point he had led a life of stellar obedience. Still, one transgression meant he was banned forever, thus proving that under the Law, one must obey all the commandments perfectly to be saved (James 2:10). If Moses the mediator did not inherit what was promised due to his failure, what chance did the rest of Israel have?

The remainder of the Old Testament proves that that was the case. It records the sad story of one failure after another, following their rebellion at Sinai during the forty years they followed the Lord in the wilderness. The journey itself, which was only to take eleven days, turned into forty years due to their continual rebellion and hardness of heart. Even Aaron's sons, who were appointed to serve as priests with their father, rebelled against God's instructions and, in an intoxicated state, offered strange fire before the Lord and were consumed by God's wrath (Leviticus 10:2).

Ten times the Israelites rebelled against him in the wilderness. The prophet Amos summed up their idolatrous habits while they sojourned those forty years:

> *Did you bring to me slain beasts and sacrifices, during the forty years in the wilderness, O house of Israel? You took up the tent of Moloch and the star of your god Rephan, the images that you made to worship; and I will send you into exile beyond Babylon.*
>
> *Acts 7:42-43*

And that's before they even came into the land of Canaan! That period (in the Promised Land) might be best described as an idolatrous free-for-all, with Israel continually playing the harlot with false gods. The book of Judges demonstrates their see-saw like existence; one minute serving God, followed by total rejection of the theocracy and asking God for a king, which God had expressly forbidden (I Samuel 8). In fact, there was no period in the entire time they lived in the land that they were obedient to God by keeping the covenant. It is a continual history of rebellion and idolatry, culminating first in God's judgment falling upon the ten northern tribes of Israel when they were carried away by the Assyrians. Over a century later in 587 B.C., the Babylonians came down to her sister Judah and destroyed the temple and city of Jerusalem. Because of God's promise that Messiah would come through the line of Judah, God preserved a remnant who would return and rebuild the temple seventy years later.

Perhaps the apostle Paul sums up best their rebellion by quoting the prophet Isaiah: "*But of Israel he says, 'All day long I have held out my hands to a disobedient and contrary people'* (Romans 10:21). Their entire history from the beginning was one of rebellion and disobedience. The deacon Stephen, while testifying before the Jewish Sanhedrin which eventually led to his death, reminded them how their long history of rebellion culminated in their rejection of the Messiah whom God sent to them: *"Which of the prophets did your fathers not persecute? And they killed those who announced beforehand the coming of the Righteous One, whom you have now betrayed and murdered, you who received the law as delivered by angels and did not keep it"* (Acts 7:52-53).

Since they rejected those who announced his coming, it is not surprising they became the betrayers and murderers of the One who was promised. This final stage of their rebellion would also culminate in the destruction of the city and temple in 70A.D., just as it did in the destruction of the first temple.

GENTILES FAILURE

Israel stood condemned before the God of Israel for their failure to keep the Law in the Old Testament. Since the Law demanded perfect obedience, they were unable to keep it. If they had kept it perfectly, they would be righteous before God. But they couldn't as David reminds us: "God looks down from heaven on the children of man to see if there are any who understand, who seek after God. They have all fallen away; together they have become corrupt; there is none who does good, *not even one* (Psalms 53:2-3, italics mine).

Not only did Israel fail to keep the Law, the Gentiles who did not have the Law in written form failed to keep it as well. How can Gentiles break the Law if they never even had it?' The apostle Paul answers that question in the second chapter of his letter to the Romans when he describes how the Law is written into the consciences of those who did not have it in written form (Romans 2:14-16). Therefore, they are judged by their attitude towards what they know to be true *within* them, even though they did not have it in written form. In other words, since the Law is the Law of God, the Creator has written it into the consciences of all men and women. The first time a child lies, he feels a twinge of guilt, even if he has never read the command, "You shall not bear false witness." So even though they did not violate a direct command which was engraved on stone, they were still guilty of breaking it since its principles were written on their hearts.

In this way, Paul establishes that the entire human race has broken the covenant. Whether pagans (Romans 1:18-32), moralists, (2:1-16) or Jews (2:17-3:9), all human being stand guilty before God and have violated it. That means there is not one human being who does not stand guilty before God. Paul summarizes it in the third chapter of Romans by saying, "*all* have sinned and fallen short of the glory of God" (Romans 3:23).

Contrasting Adam and Christ

To understand why the Old Covenant is a broken covenant, we must first understand what Paul teaches in Romans 5:12-21. There, he presents Adam and Jesus as *'federal'* heads of their prospective races. Behind the idea of *'federal head'* is that God deals with the human race in terms of *representatives*. That simply means, as goes the representative, so goes all those who are *in* him.

A good illustration of that can be seen in the familiar Old Testament story of David and Goliath. When Goliath, the champion of the Philistines touted Israel, he said, "Am I not a Philistine, and are you not servants of Saul? Choose a man for yourselves, and let him come down to me. If he is able to fight with me and kill me, then we will be your servants. But if I prevail against him and kill him, then you shall be our servants and serve us" (I Samuel 17:8-9). Goliath was saying that he was the representative of the people of Philistia; so, if Israel defeated Goliath, it meant that the entire nation was defeated and would become Israel's slaves. The same was true with whoever Israel chose; if they were defeated then the entire nation of Israel was defeated and would become slaves to the Philistines. That's because both David and Goliath represented their people and their destinies were tied up in each of them. Personal matters were not all that was at stake, but, more importantly, the destiny of an entire people.

Paul uses the same logic in Romans 5:12-21 when comparing Adam to Christ. Both were federal heads which meant that as they go, so would their descendants after them. This is a hard concept for us in the West to grasp because we tend to think in terms of our *individuality* rather than our *solidarity*. But in the ancient world as well as the East today, people think of themselves largely in terms of the community they are part of. In the East, a person forms their identity by his or her solidarity with others. And since the Bible was written in an Eastern culture, it assumes this perspective.

Part of Paul's purpose in this section is to explain the human race inherited Adam's sin and the guilt associated with it ("For as by the one man's disobedience the many were made sinners, so by the one man's obedience the many will be made righteous:" (vs. 5:19). It's not that Adam sinned and his descendants all chose to follow in his footsteps (though this is certainly true). Rather, it is Adam's sin and the guilt associated with it was passed on to all of Adam's descendants, even those who never transgressed a direct command. That's because all of his descendants were *in* him. This simply means Adam's descendants were vitally united to him when Adam sinned so that they are seen as sinning with Adam, even though technically they had not even been born.

The writer of Hebrews uses the same logic in his teaching regarding the Melchizedek priesthood, which Jesus holds (see Hebrews 7). He argues that this priesthood is superior to the Levitical priesthood, which was the priesthood serving the temple at that time. One of the ways he does that is by referring to the fact that Abraham paid tithes to Melchizedek when he met him coming back from the slaughter of the kings (Genesis 14). Since Levi, from whom the earthly priesthood comes, was *in* Abraham when he tithed to Melchizedek, this is an indication that the priesthood of Jesus (from the order of Melchizedek) is superior to that of Levi since the one who tithes does so to one who is greater than him.

The fact Adam passed on his guilt to all his descendants is evident in another way as the Apostle Paul states in Romans 5:12-14. Paul argues if Adam's sin and the resultant guilt were not passed on to his descendants, then those who lived between Adam and Moses would not have died since they had not transgressed the Law because it was not given yet. To grasp this argument, we must remember death resulted as a direct transgression of God's commands. But since those who lived between Adam and Moses had no Law to transgress, they should not have died. But what does the Apostle say? "Yet death reigned from Adam to Moses, even over those whose sinning was not like the transgression of Adam, who was a type of the one who was to come" (Romans 5:14).

In this passage, Paul teaches what theologians later termed the 'Doctrine of Original Sin.' It is the idea that we inherited not only Adam's guilt for our being in Adam, but his *nature* as well:

> *"The Fall of Adam is the "original" sin and the hereditary fallen nature and moral corruption that is passed down from Adam to his descendants. It is called "original" in that Adam, the first man, is the one who sinned and thus caused sin to enter the world. Even though Eve is the one who sinned first, because Adam is the Federal Head (representative of mankind), his fall included or represented all of humanity."*[4]

Of course, Romans 5:12-21 is not just an account of how all the human race fell in Adam but focuses also on how God has redeemed a people

---

4 *Christian Apologetics and Research Ministry*, Matt Slick, 12/10/08).

out of fallen Adam through the federal head, Christ: "For as in Adam all die, so also in Christ shall all be made alive" (I Corinthians 15:22). Paul's purpose in this section is not merely to compare Adam and Christ but to contrast them as well. If the fall of Adam wrought devastation for the human race than the obedience of Christ brought much more blessing! In Adam the Old Covenant fails, but in Christ there is a New Covenant that not only undoes what Adam did, but goes a long way to bring blessing.

SUMMING IT UP

We have seen in this chapter that the Old Covenant is a *broken* covenant. From the moment it was introduced at Sinai (though it certainly existed before), the people of God were unable to keep it. Was this a failure of the covenant? No; not at all! As the apostle Paul states clearly "the law is holy, and the commandment is holy and righteous and good" (Romans 7:12). There is nothing wrong with the Law or the covenant under which it was adopted: The problem (as we shall see in the next chapter) is not with the Law or the covenant but with the fact that we are *sinners*— men and women who have not merely a bad record but a bad *nature* as well. Listen to what Charles Leiter says about the sinner's real problem:

> "*According to the Lord Jesus Christ, man himself is corrupt and vile. 'That which proceeds out of the man, that is what defiles the man. For from within, out of the heart of man, proceed evil thoughts, fornications, thefts, murders, adulteries, deeds of coveting and wickedness, as well as deceit, sensuality, envy, slander, pride and foolishness. All these evil things proceed from within and defile the man.'" This is the condition of every human heart, apart from Christ. If a motion picture or even our past thoughts, let alone our*

past actions, were to be played on a large screen before our family and acquaintances, every one of us would run from the room in shame. Every non-Christian is—in his person—more repulsive to a holy God than he can ever begin to imagine'" [5]

According to the New Testament, the Law was not given as a means by which men and women could be saved but as the means to expose sin. The next chapter explores this more fully.

5 *Justification and Regeneration*, Charles Lieter, page 21.

CHAPTER THREE

WHY THE OLD COVENANT WAS GIVEN

Roy Hession, in his classic work on the epistle to the Hebrews, *From Shadow to Substance*[6], uses the following illustration to demonstrate what God designed his Law to do. I am not quoting it verbatim but highlighting it as best as I can recall it:

A man was strolling through a field one summer day when suddenly he came upon a bull sleeping peacefully in a field. His initial impression (mistakenly) was that the bull was a peaceful, gentle animal. Suddenly, the man goes to the trunk of his car and takes out a red blanket. Standing fifty feet in front of the bull, he begins waving it frantically. The bull, which was sleeping peacefully, now awakens and becomes a raging beast, snorting and charging the man, intent on destroying him.

The question Hession poses is, *"Did the red blanket change the nature of the bull?"* The answer, of course, is 'No.' All the blanket did was to reveal the

---

6 Hession, R. (1977). *From shadow to substance: A rediscovery of the inner message of the Epistle to the Hebrews focused on the words 'Let us go on'.* Alresford: Christian Literature Crusade.

bull's true nature. While sleeping peacefully in the field gave the impression the bull was a benign creature, its real nature is that of a raging beast. All the blanket did was to bring to light what was really there. In other words, the blanket revealed who the bull *really* was.

The point Hession makes by using this illustration is that in the same way the red blanket exposed the true nature of the bull, so God designed the Law to bring out our true nature as *sinners*. Apart from the Law, human beings are able to hide their *true* nature in the same way the bull did by sleeping peacefully in the field. But when the Law comes and we are judged in the light of what it says, we suddenly discover we have rebelled against all that is holy, righteous and good. The Law arouses sin in us "in order that sin might be shown to be sin" (Romans 7:13). So instead of helping us, the Law only condemns us by clearly exposing we are rebels. And that is what it is supposed to do, for "through the law comes knowledge of sin" (Romans 3:20).

Paul makes this even clearer when discussing his own relationship to the Law before his conversion in the seventh chapter of Romans. He says that he was "once alive apart from the Law" (Romans 7:9). What he means by this is that there was a time when he had no consciousness of the sin of covetousness (the particular sin Paul dealt with). Yet once he was made aware of the commandment ("you shall not covet"), Paul says, "sin *came alive* and I died" (7:9, emphasis added). In other words, until the Law came he was blind to his sin, but the moment he was made aware of the commandment, he became conscious of his sin and by it was slain (not physically but spiritually):

"Yet if it had not been for the law, I would not have known sin. For I would not have known what it is to covet if the law had not said, 'You shall not covet.' But sin, seizing an opportunity through the commandment, produced in me all kinds of covetousness. For apart from the law, sin lies dead. I was once alive apart from the law, but when the commandment came, sin came alive and I died. The very commandment that promised life proved to be death to me.

For sin, seizing an opportunity through the commandment, deceived me and through it killed me" (Romans 7:7-11).

So, the Law operates like a mirror, exposing sin. Without the Law we are not aware of the presence of sin, but the moment we are brought face to face with the Law, it reveals that we are transgressors. And that results in our *death* which is always the penalty for sin— spiritual death, which means the loss of relationship with God. The problem therefore is not with the Law but that we are sinners. The Law is simply the means whereby our sin is brought to light. Without it, we would not know what sin is.

IGNORANT OF GOD'S RIGHTEOUSNESS

It is vital that we understand that the Old Covenant was never intended to be the means of achieving righteousness, but the instrument through which we gain knowledge of sin. When Paul says that *"by works of the law no human being will be justified in his sight"* (Romans 3:20), he is saying if a person keeps the Law perfectly, he can obtain righteousness. But the reality is because of our sin, we are not able to keep the Law and thus cannot obtain righteousness.

Therefore, the Law condemns us rather than exonerates our guilt. Because we are sinners, we are Law-*breakers* rather than Law-keepers. Thus, if justification is based on perfect obedience to the Law, there is no way a human being could achieve it.

Over the last two decades, there has been much debate over whether or not first-century Jewish religion was legalistic, teaching Torah-observance as essential for salvation. But the record of Scripture seems clear that first century Pharisees viewed it this way. Paul himself, described his former life as a Pharisee in Philippians 3:1-9, as he tells of his previous attempt to be blameless under the Law. Using the word *gain* in Philippians 3:7, a word translated from a Greek term from which we derive the idea of a miser, we can visualize Paul as a man sitting in front of a scale in which both his good deeds and bad deeds were being weighed. For Paul, as long as, his good deeds outweighed his bad, he was assured that he lived a righteous life. So, he regularly made deposits in the 'good' column through Torah observance so as to tip the scales.

That this was the essence of Pharisaical Judaism can be seen from the statement of the apostle that Israel was *"ignorant of God's righteousness"* and went about *"seeking to establish their own"* (Romans 10:3). That is what the apostle meant when he said they *"stumbled over the stumbling stone"* (9:32). No man could achieve righteousness through the Law. However, when man submitted, God extended righteousness as a gift (Romans10:3). But Israel was ignorant of this, because they believed they could obtain righteousness through their own works.

THE KNOWLEDGE OF SIN

Therefore, God never gave the Law as a means of obtaining salvation or achieving righteousness. The true purpose of the Law was to make us know we are Law-breakers and, therefore, helpless to obtain righteousness before God. And knowing that is essential to understanding what the New Covenant is all about.

This is why the Apostle Paul, when comparing the two covenants, refers to the Old as both the "ministry of death, carved in letters on stone" and the "ministry of condemnation" (II Corinthians 3:7). We should not understand these statements to mean that the first covenant is not from God. In fact, Paul is careful to remind them it was given from God and came with a certain glory (3:9). But the end result of the first covenant was condemnation and death because all who tried to live under it were brought to judgment (II Corinthians 3:7). That is why the apostle Paul says, "the law brings wrath" (Romans 4:15). Under the first covenant we are transgressors and therefore deserving of the wrath of God. The Law simply magnifies the offense by proving we are *"children of wrath"* (Ephesians 2:3).

I was once on a flight returning from a long ministry week when I struck up a conversation with a man sitting next to me. Something told me he was Jewish and after exchanging a few niceties, I learned he was. In the course of the conversation, he asked me what I did. To properly answer a fellow-Jew who asks what I do, I always feel the need to first explain what I believe. So, I took a few minutes to tell him I was a Jew who believed in Jesus as our Messiah and gave him some basic reasons why I believed in Him. Then it was my time to ask him what he did. When I did, he hesitated and sheepishly said, "You're not going to like it. I own several pornographic bookstores in Philadelphia."

I will never forget the conversation which followed. After telling me what business he was in, he then preceded to tell me he was a practicing Jew who had a relationship with God. Slowly, the conversation turned to the Torah and I began to walk him through each of the ten commandments. As I was approaching the sixth ("you shall not commit adultery") he suddenly stopped me and said, "I know where this is going." With that, the conversation promptly ended and for the remainder of the flight he acted as if I wasn't there.

What had happened? This man instinctively knew that he was violating the sixth commandment in owning and operating adult book stores. Therefore, he refused to engage me, on the basis of that commandment, which exposed his sin. The Law did its work in convicting him of his sin.

During his earthly ministry, Jesus demonstrated the Law is the means by which knowledge of sin is given when he dealt with a rich young ruler. This man inquired of Jesus as to what he must *do* to inherit eternal life (Matthew 19:16-22). It is important to note that for this man, eternal life was the result of something he *did*. In the light of this question, our Lord responded to this man. Instead of giving him the gospel, Jesus told him that if he kept the commandments, he would inherit eternal life (vs: 17-19). When the man asked which commandments, Jesus recited those from the second tablet which describe one's duty to others, coupled with the positive command, "You shall love your neighbor as yourself."

At first glance, this is confusing because it seems Jesus taught the rich young ruler salvation is by Torah observance, which is contradictory to the Gospel. Yet upon closer inspection, we see Jesus, the Master-Teacher, was not teaching salvation by Torah observance at all. Rather, he used the Law for what it was intended to do: to convict this young man of sin so that he would come to Christ *alone* for salvation. The young man, having no consciousness of having violated any of the commandments, asked what he now lacked. Jesus, knowing that this man coveted riches, essentially took him to the tenth command when he told him to "go, sell what you possess and give to the poor, and you will have treasure in heaven; and come, follow me" (Matthew 19:21). While not quoting the tenth commandment directly, Jesus is in fact demonstrating he had broken it by his unwillingness to part with his money. He walked away sad because he loved his money more than Jesus. Therefore, Jesus demonstrated by his use of the Law how it serves as the instrument which exposed sin.

But not only does the Law of Moses expose our sin, the principle of *law* does so as well. Do you remember when you were young and your mom put a plate of cookies on the counter with the command, "Don't touch those till after dinner?" What happened? The minute she issued the command, you found yourself craving the cookies. If she had offered no prohibition you probably would have ignored the command, but the moment the command went forth, it produced in you all kinds of cravings to reach for the cookies.

Why are we tempted to disobey commands when they are given? The answer extends back to the beginning of time, when Adam and Eve were first placed in the Garden of Eden. There, God placed them in a perfect environment with everything they would ever need. The only restriction was that they must avoid eating from the tree of the knowledge of good and evil. This single restriction must be seen in the light of the lavish freedom they had to eat from all the other trees in the Garden (see Genesis 2:16-17). Why did they ignore the gracious provision of eating from every tree freely in order to violate the one restriction that had been put on them?

Scripture only tells us that the serpent deceived Eve into thinking that the tree they were forbidden to eat from was really the one that would bring them life. We must remember that at this point Adam and Eve had no sin nature to tempt them. That is not true of us, as James reminds us when he says, *"each person is tempted when he is lured and enticed by his own desire"* (James 1:14).

Paul speaks of our 'sinful passions being aroused by the law' in Romans 7. So, we find it a principle of our fallen nature that the law arouses our sin so that we want to violate the command that has been given.

———————————

The Law, our Guardian

Under the Old Covenant, the Law served the purpose of being a *guardian*, a word translated from the Greek word *'paidagogos'* (Galatians 3:24). Here is how the Mounce Greek Dictionary[7] describes a *paidagogos*:

> *"a person, usually a slave or freedman, to whom the care of the boys of a family was committed, whose duty it was to attend them at their play, lead them to and from the public school, and exercise a constant superintendence over their conduct and safety; in NT an ordinary director or minister contrasted with an Apostle, as a pedagogue occupies an inferior position to a parent, 1 Cor. 4:15; a term applied to the Mosaic law, as dealing with men as in a state of mere childhood and tutelage."*

As Mounce states, a paidagogos is the term for a slave in the Roman world whose job it was to prepare children for adulthood. He was responsible for their education and for training them to become mature adults. Once the children came of age, they would no longer be under the schoolmaster, having graduated from his care. In the same way, the apostle Paul compares the Law of Moses to a *'paidagogos'*. John Calvin, in his Galatian commentary points out the similarities:

> *"The comparison applies in both respects to the law, for its authority was limited to a particular age, and its whole object was to prepare its scholars in such a manner, that, when its elementary instructions were closed, they might make progress worthy of manhood"*

---

7 Mounce, William D. *Mounce's Completed Expository Dictionary of Old and New Testament.*

So, the apostle in comparing the Law to a guardian, implies that it was necessary for our education and discipline "until Christ came in order that we may be justified by faith" (Galatians 3:24). That means that once the Law had served its purpose, it would be done away with. It was given as the means of preparing us to be justified by faith. Once the One had come to whom the promises had been made, there was no longer a need for a schoolmaster.

That does not mean that the Law has no present value. Indeed, it does, if, as Paul says, "one uses it lawfully" (I Timothy 1:8). We have much to learn from the Old Covenant if we interpret it in the light of the New. Yet, once Messiah appeared, the guardian was no longer necessary.

CHAPTER FOUR

THE COVENANT OF GRACE

My wife and I don't go to the movies often but when we do we both like different things. For example, she insists on not missing any of the previews while I despise them and can't wait till they're over, so the movie can begin. If I had my druthers, I would skip them entirely. But I sit through them because I enjoy being with my wife.

In the same way that movie previews pique our interest to want to see the movie, so God gave previews in the Old Testament of the coming New Covenant. Like big screen movie previews, these glimpses into the future were usually short, prophetic unveilings meant to prepare the faithful for the good things that lie ahead. For example, many previews of Messiah's atoning death were given for centuries through the Old Testament prophets. I will never forget the impact on my soul when, as a Jew, I read for the first time the fifty third chapter of Isaiah; that great chapter setting forth the substitutionary death of Messiah for Israel. Since I had never learned to read and understand the Hebrew text of the Old Testament, I had never actually read this chapter.

But just before my conversion, someone gave me a Gospel tract containing the English text of this great prophecy. It was greatly used by God in convincing me that Jesus was my Messiah who died for me.

A Covenant of Grace

God gave one of clearest previews of the New Covenant to his people during the life of Abraham. When God first called Abram out of the land of the Chaldeans, he promised him, *"in you all the families of the earth shall be blessed"* (Genesis 12:3). At the time this promise was given though, Abram was seventy-five and still childless. How could all the nations of the earth be blessed through an old man who was yet to bear children? After Abram had rescued his nephew Lot from the slaughter of the kings (Genesis 14), God spoke to Abram and reminded him that he would give him divine protection (15:1). Again, Abram responded by reminding the Lord he remained childless and that his heir was the servant in his house. That's when God spoke and promised him a son from his own loins:

> *And behold, the word of the Lord came to him: "This man shall not be your heir; your very own son shall be your heir." And he brought him outside and said, "Look toward heaven, and number the stars, if you are able to number them." Then he said to him, "So shall your offspring be.*
>
> Gen. 15:4-5

To reconfirm the promise, God took Abram outside and told him lift up his eyes to heaven and to count the stars if possible. If it were impossible for Abram to number the stars, so it would be impossible for him to number his offspring. What could Abram do? Even if he began to produce offspring from that moment how could he fulfill this promise? All he could do was trust the God who made this promise, which is exactly what the text said he did: *"And he believed the Lord, and he counted it to him as righteousness"* (15:6).

Abram knew he could not fulfill the promise in his own power, yet he also knew that he was dealing with God who made the promise. So, he *"believed the Lord"* and God considered his faith to be *righteousness*. It is from this verse that Paul derived his understanding of the great doctrine of Justification by Faith Alone (Galatians 3:6). In Romans 4, he tells us that, despite Abraham's bodily limitations and the deadness of Sarah's womb (see Romans 4:18-21), he believed that God would fulfill his promise. And according to the apostle, the statement that God *"counted it to him as righteousness"* was written not just for Abraham's sake, but for ours as well (4:24). When we believe that God raised Jesus from the dead, our faith is counted as righteousness to us as well.

While Abraham believed that God would fulfill his promise regarding offspring, he was not as confident that God would fulfill his promise to give him the land (Genesis 15:7-8). When Abraham asked for a confirmation that God was indeed giving it to him, he was instructed to bring a three-year-old heifer, a female goat, a ram, a turtle dove, and a young pigeon for sacrifice. Abraham, according to custom, divided these (except for the birds) and laid the pieces across from one another in accordance with the practice of cutting a covenant, in which each party, after dividing the pieces, would pass through them, reciting the covenantal terms.

But as Abraham waited for God to pass between the pieces so that he might follow, the Lord laid a deep sleep upon him and a terror descended on him (15:12). It was then that God spoke to him, announcing beforehand what would happen to his descendants; that they would be *"sojourners in a land that is not theirs*" and that they would be *"afflicted for four hundred years*" (15:13). But afterwards, God would bring judgment on the nation they served, and they would come out with great possessions. All of this was fulfilled, of course, during that entire period Israel was in bondage to Egypt and the subsequent exodus from that land. As God had said to Abraham, Israel vanquished their enemies and left Egypt with great possessions.

After sleeping for most of the day, Abraham awakened and saw a "smoking fire pot and a flaming torch passed between these pieces" (15:17). These were all tokens of the divine presence, and as they passed through the pieces, the voice of God was heard announcing the covenantal terms:

> *"To your offspring I give this land, from the river of Egypt to the great river, the river Euphrates, the land of the Kenites, the Kenizzites, the Kadmonites, the Hittites, the Perizzites, the Rephaim, the Amorites, the Canaanites, the Girgashites and the Jebusites" (15:18-21)*

Here, God is reaffirming his promise to give Abraham and his descendants the land. But if we look carefully, there is one thing missing from this story: Abraham himself never passed between the pieces. Only God did. What does this mean? It means that the covenant was not a conditional covenant dependent on Abraham's obedience, but an unconditional one, dependent on God alone. In other words, when God entered this covenant with Abraham, he didn't enter it with Abraham—he entered it with himself! If Abraham would have passed through the pieces, then he would have been responsible to hold up his end of the bargain. But since he did not, there was nothing to uphold.

This indicates that the covenant God entered with Abraham was a covenant of *grace*. It was not dependent on what Abraham would do or could do but upon what God had promised. This was, in fact, an early foreshadowing of the *New* Covenant. In fact, the only way that men and women were saved in both the Old and New Testament periods was by believing in the *New* Covenant. That's why the apostle Paul, at the end of Romans four says, "the words 'it was counted to him' were not written for his sake alone, but for ours also. It will be counted to us who believe in him who raised from the dead Jesus our Lord, who was delivered up for our trespasses and raised for our justification" (4:23-25).

THE GREAT HALL OF FAITH

The eleventh chapter of Hebrews has been called the Great Hall of Faith. That is the list of Old Testament persons who had faith in the promise of the coming Messiah. It is important to realize that the writer of Hebrews is not merely saying that these men and women had faith in God in a general sense. Rather, each one had faith God would send his Son to redeem them. Regardless of what they had to deal with or what it cost them, each one clung to the promise of God's redeeming faith.

Take, for example, what the writer says about Cain and Abel in Hebrews 11:4:

> *"By faith Abel offered to God a more acceptable sacrifice than Cain, through which he was commended as righteous, God commending him by accepting his gifts. And through his faith, though he died, he still speaks."*

How did Abel know to bring God a sacrifice that would please him? It is due to the fact he believed the promise of the need for a coming Savior as evidenced by his awareness that the earth now lies under a curse and that only blood would atone. Cain, on the other hand, disregarded the curse and brought to God the fruit of his hands. So, Abel's faith was more than a generalized faith in God; He believed the Gospel that only blood would be acceptable to God and that God would accept him because of it. Cain did not believe the Gospel and thus believed that his own works were acceptable to God. Consequently, his approach to God was not accepted and his sins were not covered.

We have already seen how Abraham was justified by faith in the fourth chapter of Romans. Here, in Hebrews 11, Abraham's obedience is seen as the fruit of his faith, causing him to look beyond his immediate circumstances for a city which God had built:

> "By faith Abraham obeyed when he was called to go out to a place that he was to receive as an inheritance. And he went out, not knowing where he was going. By faith he went to live in the land of promise, as in a foreign land, living in tents with Isaac and Jacob, heirs with him of the same promise. For he was looking forward to the city that has foundations, whose designer and builder is God."
>
> *Hebrews 11:6-10*

Many others are listed in the Great Hall of Faith who, through faith,

> "conquered kingdoms, enforced justice, obtained promises, stopped the mouths of lions, quenched the power of fire, escaped the edge of the sword, were made strong out of weakness, became mighty in war, put foreign armies to flight. Women received back their dead

by resurrection. Some were tortured, refusing to accept release, so that they might rise again to a better life. Others suffered mocking and flogging, and even chains and imprisonment. They were stoned, they were sawn in two, they were killed with the sword. They went about in skins of sheep and goats, destitute, afflicted, mistreated—of whom the world was not worthy—wandering about in deserts and mountains, and in dens and caves of the earth" (11:32-38).

These men and women were not justified and made right with God by their works, but by their faith. This is the only way that people have ever been made right with God. This list (along with many others not mentioned) is of those who *believed* the Gospel in their day, although Messiah had not yet come. Their faith looked *forward* to the day of its fulfillment:

"And all these, though commended through their faith, did not receive what was promised, since God had provided something better for us, that apart from us they should not be made perfect" (11: 39-40).

PROMISE, LAW, GRACE

We have seen in the previous chapter that the Law was given as a means of exposing our sin so as to prepare us for the Gospel. What is the relationship between the Law and the covenant of grace made with Abraham in Genesis 15?

To answer that, this is a good time to pull back so as to gain an overview of how the covenant with Abraham relates to the Law and foreshadows the grace which was to come in the Messiah. The best way to understand this is by relating three words together: *promise, law,* and *grace.*

We start with *promise* because it is the best word to describe the covenant God made with Abraham in Genesis 15. As we have seen, God promised to give Abraham a child through whom he would have descendants more numerous than the stars of the heavens. This is the promise which Abraham believed (though he had no visible assurance) and by which he was justified. And it is this promise by which we are justified as well. All the true sons of Abraham are sons (including daughters) through faith in the promise.

We have already seen in the previous chapter that between the giving of the promise and its fulfillment, the *Law* came in to increase the transgression (to make sin appear even more sinful). The fulfillment of the promise could not be dependent on keeping the Law, because then it would not be based on promise. "Why then the law? It was added because of transgressions, until the offspring should come to whom the promise had been made, and it was put in place through angels by an intermediary" (Galatians 3:19). Notice how Paul ties in the Law to the fulfillment of the promise. The Law was never meant to be permanent, but only in place until the offspring of Abraham appeared. When Paul says it was "added because of transgressions", he means that the purpose of the Law was to convict the world of its sin in order to make sin appear exceedingly sinful.

But Law was given to prepare the people for the *grace* which has come in Christ Jesus. The covenant with Abraham had foreshadowed this grace in that it was made with Abraham on the basis of promise and not law. Therefore, because the promise is not dependent on obeying the Law but on faith, it is by grace:

> *"That is why it depends on faith, in order that the promise may rest on grace and be guaranteed to all his offspring—not only to the adherent of the law but also to the one who shares the faith of Abraham, who is the father of us all."*
>
> *Romans 4:16*

Promise, law, and grace are perhaps the best way to look at the entire Bible. It lays out how the promise made to Abraham was given before the Law so that it governed all of God's dealings with those he would redeem. The Law came in because it was the means of exposing sin and thus preparing people for redemption of Messiah through his blood. And the result is that grace might now be given to each believer in the New Covenant.

Chapter Five

The New Covenant
Isn't Written

One of my favorite scenes from any movie is the scene in The Ten Commandments where God gives Moses the two tablets of the Law on Mount Sinai. While it seems a little cheesy now, it was really done well for the time. As each word proceeds from his mouth, the fire of God smites the tablets and the words are permanently engraved. As the scene ends, Moses carries the tablets of the Law down the holy mount to deliver them to the people, only to find that the people he brought out of Egypt had already gone whoring after other gods.

As a Jew, I grew up hearing the story of the Exodus and how our people were adopted by God at Mount Sinai. Over a million people (six hundred thousand men many of whom were married and had kids) heard the audible voice of God speaking the ten words (commandments) out of the midst of the Mount as it burned with fire (Exodus 20:22). The people were awestruck! Consequently, they did not want another word spoken! (I've sat under preaching like that). Moses himself trembled in his boots (sandals) and was terrified (see Hebrews 12:19-21).

But without a doubt the highlight of the story was when God wrote the ten words on stone tablets with his own finger. There is only one word to describe it, the very word Paul uses: *'glory'* (II Corinthians 3:7-8). Such a manifestation of God's glory was unparalleled in the Old Testament era. Future generations of Israelites were to look back at this signal event by which God's glory was revealed to Israel. No other people on earth were privileged to hear the voice of the living God speaking from the midst of the fire and lived to tell about it (Deuteronomy 4:32-36). Talk about glory.

Yet Paul says that the former glory revealed at Sinai has now faded in the light of the glory which has come with the dawning of the New Covenant (II Corinthians 3:7-11). Did you get that? *In the broken, bloody, battered body of the Lord Jesus on the cross of Calvary and his subsequent resurrection, a glory is revealed which far exceeds the glory which accompanied the inaugurating of the Old Covenant!* There are many reasons for this but the main one is that while the glory of that first covenant was manifest when God wrote his laws on tablets of stone, the glory of the New Covenant is that God now writes his laws, not on stone, but on the fleshly tablets of human hearts. In other words, the New Covenant isn't primarily written in an external form but deeply engraved into human hearts by the sovereign work of the Spirit of God.

PERFECT EXPRESSION OF
THE NATURE OF GOD

In the great prophecy of the New Covenant (Jeremiah 31:31-34), God declares the covenant he will make with them will not be *"like the covenant that I made with their fathers on the day when I took them by the hand to bring them out of the land of Egypt, my covenant that they broke, though I was their husband, declares the Lord"* (vs. 32, emphasis mine). The words, "not be like the covenant" describe how this *New* Covenant differs from the old which it replaces. Let me explain.

The Old Covenant was an *external* law written on tablets of stone which regulated the behavior of the people of God. That is how the majority of people still think of these commandments today—as regulations governing outward behavior and curbing sin. It has been pointed out before the Ten Commandments are written as negatives (you shall not steal, you shall not commit adultery, you shall not bear false witness, etc.). They are written that way because we are sinners and it is our propensity to do the very things the commandments forbid. So, the commandments need to be very direct in prohibiting those behaviors contrary to God's will.

But there is another way of viewing these commandments, not only as a means by which sin is curbed, but also as the vehicle through which we learn who God is and what He is like. If we want to know what God is like, we should study the Ten Commandments. For example, the commandment, *"You shall not bear false witness"* on the surface, tell us it is a sin to lie. But the question should be asked, *"Why is it a sin to lie?"* The answer is, to lie is to sin against truth. But the question we should obviously ask next is, "What is *truth*?" In Scripture, truth is not an ideal or a moral system or a philosophy, but a Person! We know One who said, *"I am the way, the truth, and the life"* (John 14:6). So, if I lie to you, I am sinning against you, but I am ultimately sinning against truth which means I am sinning against God. In this way, each of the Ten Commandments, though certainly curbing sinful behavior, reveals something about the nature of God.

If the Law then is the perfect expression of the nature of God, why was it necessary to bring a *New* Covenant into being? The reason is, the Old Covenant, since it was an external code written on stone, could not be kept by sinful human beings. It brought judgment and death since a curse rested on everyone who did not keep all of its precepts. The problem therefore was not with the covenant, but the frailty and weakness of those trying to keep it.

So, in view of this (that sinful men and women could not keep the Law), God spoke to Israel through Jeremiah that one day he would bring in an entirely *new* way of bringing people into relationship with God. It would be different from the Old Covenant for the simple reason that whereas the Old Covenant was written on tablets of stone, the New Covenant wouldn't be written at all (at least not on stone or paper with ink).

Some may protest the previous statement that the New Covenant isn't written by referring to the second half of our Bible we call the New Testament. I agree the second half of our Bible we call the New Testament was written by men who put pen to paper (or stylus to papyri). But the New Covenant God made with his people is not a written code in the same sense that the Old Covenant was. It is (as the apostle Paul clearly states), "written *not with ink* but with the Spirit of the living God, not on *tablets of stone* but on *tablets of human hearts*" (II Corinthians 3:3, emphasis mine).

Did you get that? This covenant is not like the Old Covenant which was written on tablets of stone. That's because it is written *internally* on tablets of human hearts. This has incredible implications for how God intends for us to live the Christian life. First and foremost, it means that God's righteousness is not merely an external standard, but an inward reality.

AN INNER RIGHTEOUSNESS

When First Century Jews thought of righteous and holy people they almost always thought of the scribes and Pharisees. So, when Jesus told his disciples in the Sermon on the Mount their righteousness had to exceed that of the scribes and Pharisees, they must have been totally blown away (Matthew 5:20). How could they possibly exceed their righteousness since they fasted, prayed, studied Torah all the time and avoided coming in contact with sinners? Could they possibly be more righteous than that?

But Jesus in this Sermon wasn't calling them to a righteousness that was greater than that of the scribes and Pharisees in terms of *outward* observances but in terms of *inward* change. After making that statement (that their righteousness had to exceed that of the scribes and Pharisees), Jesus gave several examples to illustrate what he meant which are commonly called the Antithesis (Matthew 5:21-48). Jesus isn't adding to the Law in these statements, but uncovering the Law's real meaning. It was never meant merely to govern outward performance, but uncover the real condition of human hearts.

For example, the scribes and Pharisees viewed the command prohibiting adultery as dealing only with the outward act itself (5:27-30). But Jesus teaches the original intent of the Law was not merely dealing with the act itself but demonstrated our adulterous hearts. The righteousness, which exceeds the scribes and Pharisees, begins with purity in the heart. This is what is meant when He says their righteousness must exceed that of the scribes and Pharisees.

This fact (that the Law really dealt with what was within) helps us to understand why it was necessary for God to bring in a *New* Covenant. Something more was needed than an external code written on stone. And that is what is promised in the New Covenant: *"I will put my law within them, and write it on their hearts"* (Jeremiah 3:33). The righteousness of the New Covenant is not obtained by adhering to an outward code but by an inward law. God literally writes his laws on our hearts so that we now live by the power of a transformed heart.

An illustration from marriage helps to understand this. By God's grace I have never committed the act of adultery when it comes to honoring my marriage vows. But I have refrained from it not because of an outward command regulating my behavior, but because of an inward law of *love*. The truth is, I don't want to commit it because I am head over heels in love with my wife. So, I obey the commandment not to commit adultery, not because of an outward law which tells me not to do it, but because of a heart drawn to my wife (she still makes my heart flutter).

This is what Jesus meant when he told the disciples that they needed a righteousness which exceeded that of the religious leaders of his day. He was dealing with their need for a righteousness that was *qualitatively* not *quantitatively* different. In other words, Jesus was not telling us that we needed to perform more righteous acts than the scribes and Pharisees, but exhibit a righteousness that issues from a transformed heart. And that transformed heart is a result of the New Covenant and God's promise to "put his law within us and write it on our hearts."

I am not suggesting at all this inward righteousness does not reveal itself in changed behavior, for it most certainly does. Before I was saved, I cursed like a sailor but once the Spirit of God wrote his laws on my heart, I found I couldn't curse anymore. When I did, I felt a deep sense of grieving I never felt before. What had changed? The Spirit of God had done an *inward* work so that my behavior now reflected the law of God, not as an outward code, but an inner life. It was the result of the miracle of *regeneration*.

More Than A Written Document

So, the New Covenant is not essentially a *written* document in the same way the Old Covenant is. We are in danger if we approach the New Testament in the same way as the Old Testament, as letters written on stone. Rather, it is a written record of what life is like when it is lived under the New Covenant.

It is possible for us to learn what the New Testament teaches while all the while remaining strangers to the life of the New Covenant, approaching it as a written code we must keep in order to please God. I have known people who used the New Testament to bludgeon people about their mode of baptism or condemn them for certain practices. In this way, they demonstrate that they do not understand the New Covenant.

The New Covenant therefore is more than a written document but a spiritual covenant by which we are changed inwardly. By the means of a changed nature, we now want to keep the Law of God. That's why it isn't written with ink but with the Spirit of the Living God, not on tablets of stone, but on fleshly hearts. More about that in the next chapter.

CHAPTER SIX

THE NEW COVENANT *IS* WRITTEN

The New Testament records God's gift to the church on the Day of Pentecost; he sent the Holy Spirit (Acts 2:1). That is significant because the Jewish people believe the Day of Pentecost was also the day when Israel received the Law on Mount Sinai. The word Pentecost means *'fifty'* and was celebrated fifty days after the Sabbath of Passover week. They were to count seven Sabbaths and the day after that seventh Sabbath (Sunday) was the Day of Pentecost. It was also known as the Feast of Harvest in that it celebrated the first harvest of the year. If you read chapters thirteen through nineteen of the book of Exodus it confirms the claim that fifty days after Passover, Moses was on Mount Sinai, receiving the Law of God.

But what Moses received that day were laws engraved on stone tablets. We have already seen that man was unable to keep the Law, not because of a failure of the Law but because of our sinful nature. In Romans seven, Paul described how his repeated attempts to keep the Law only led him to frustration and failure so that he cried out, *"Who shall deliver me from this body of death"?* (Romans 7:24). The Old Covenant was powerless to deliver him (and us) from his wretched state. Something else was needed; a way in which the Law would be more than an outward code but become an inward life. Nothing less than another Pentecost was needed.

Written in our Hearts

Fast forward from that first Pentecost when Moses received stone tablets with the Law of God engraved on them to the Day of Pentecost after Jesus died at Passover, rose from the dead, and ascended to the Father forty days later. One hundred and twenty disciples are gathered in a room observing the day as other Jews (Acts 2:1). Suddenly, the room was filled with the sound of a rushing mighty wind and the disciples were filled with the glorified Spirit. Luke describes it in the second chapter of Acts:

> *"And suddenly there came from heaven a sound like a mighty rushing wind, and it filled the entire house where they were sitting. And divided tongues as of fire appeared to them and rested on each one of them. And they were all filled with the Holy Spirit and began to speak in other tongues as the Spirit gave them utterance."*
>
> *Acts 2:2-4*

Some see this as merely an account of Jesus empowering his disciples for witness. Receiving the Spirit certainly did empower them to take the Gospel to the ends of the earth. But Pentecost was much more than an empowering for mission: It was that moment when the first disciples of Jesus experienced the New Covenant. Jesus died and rose again in order to inaugurate the New

Covenant, but it wasn't until the Spirit of God entered these disciples and wrote God's Law on their hearts, that it became fully activated. This is what Paul means when he tells the Corinthian church:

"You show that you are a letter from Christ delivered by us, written not with ink but with the Spirit of the living God, not on tablets of stone but on tablets of human hearts."

II Corinthians 3:3

Just as Israel was brought into covenant at Sinai when the Law was engraved on stone, so also the 'Israel of God' came into existence when the New Covenant was written on human hearts. No longer was belonging to the people of God a matter of external conformity, but having the Law written on the heart (Romans 2:28, Galatians 6:10). This was a fulfillment of the promise given to Ezekiel centuries ago in which God promised to take away the stony heart and give his people a heart of flesh:

"And I will give you a new heart, and a new spirit I will put within you. And I will remove the heart of stone from your flesh and give you a heart of flesh. And I will put my Spirit within you, and cause you to walk in my statutes and be careful to obey my rules."

Ezekiel 36:26-27

So, the Day of Pentecost is an actual day in which God fulfilled his promise spoken through Jeremiah to put his law "within them" and "write it on their hearts." It is an important part of redemptive history like the crucifixion, resurrection and ascension. Yet it was not just for them. This miracle of the Law being written upon the hearts and minds occurs every time a person is born of the Spirit. In that moment, the Law moves from being an external code written on stone to an inward guidance system, shaping the desires and behaviors.

The previous chapter teaches the New Covenant *isn't* a written document in the same way the Old Covenant is. Having said that, let me now seemingly contradict myself by saying the New Covenant *is* written, yet not outwardly on stone or with pen and ink but on tablets of human hearts (II Corinthians 3:3). The power of the New Covenant is that God writes his laws into the fabric of our inner lives. The Law, which was engraved on stone, is now, by an operation of the Spirit of God, written on human hearts so that we obey it not as an outward code, but as an inward life.

That is why the apostle Paul tells the Corinthians that the New Covenant has a glory which far exceeds that of the old. Since the Old Covenant is a "ministry of death", the "ministry of life" is so much more glorious (II Corinthians 3:7-8). There is no possible comparison between the ministry of condemnation (the Law) and the ministry that brings righteousness (under grace). Indeed, what once had glory fades in comparison to the glory that has now come in the New Covenant (vs. 9-10).

For Paul to say that is simply amazing. How can the New Covenant with its message that the Jewish Messiah was crucified far outweigh the glory of the Old Covenant as administered by Moses on Sinai? The answer is found in the fact that it so changes us from *within*, we now keep the Law as a matter of a transformed nature rather than an outward code. We obey no longer out of fear of punishment, but because the righteousness of the Law is written in our inner life. This is accomplished in two phases; first, through the initial new *birth* whereby God initially changes our hearts, and secondly, through the ongoing work of sanctification which requires our fullest cooperation.

THE MIRACLE OF REGENERATION

In his book *Justification and Regeneration,* author Charles Leiter points out that in saving us, God must deal with two basic problems: Our bad record and our bad nature (*Justification and Regeneration,* page 33). Our bad record is dealt with by justification whereby God declares our record expunged, removing the guilt of our sin and putting his Son's righteousness in our account. But our bad *nature* cannot be dealt with by declaring us righteous: For that, God must make us entirely *new* by writing his Law on our hearts. This first work is known as *regeneration* and it is followed by the work of *sanctification.*

The great prophecy of Ezekiel 36:25-28 promised both of these works of God. Justification was foreseen in the words, *"I will sprinkle clean water on you, and you shall be clean from all your uncleannesses, and from all your idols I will cleanse you"* (Ezekiel 36:25). The term "sprinkle clean water on you" is a reference to the ritual cleansing required under the Old Covenant whereby a worshipper was declared cleansed after being sprinkled with blood and water (Hebrews 9:19). Paul pulls on this idea when he speaks of salvation as a washing in Ephesians 5:26 and Titus 3:5.

But in the next few passages in Ezekiel 36 (vs. 26-27), the prophet describes the work of the Spirit in dealing with our old nature. For that, God does a creative work that is nothing less than a miracle! We should notice that there are two aspects to this creative work of God. First, there is the replacement of the heart of hardness with a heart that is pliable and sensitive. *'Hardness of heart'* is a good description of our condition before the miracle or regeneration takes place (Ephesians 4:18). In regeneration, God removes this hardness by giving us a *new* heart and a *new* spirit (Ezekiel 36:26). That we are in desperate need of this new heart and spirit is evident by God's description of us as having a *"heart of stone."* Simply stated, our hearts are so hard we cannot respond to God without his work of removing the hardness and giving us a heart of flesh.

After he has removed the heart of stone and given us this heart of flesh, he then makes our hearts his dwelling place by putting his Spirit within us. All Christians have this indwelling Spirit residing within them or else they are not believers (Romans 8:9). At regeneration, the Holy Spirit removes the hardness of heart and puts his Spirit within them as a 'deposit' (down payment) signifying that they belong to Him and will one day receive the full inheritance.

All of this occurs instantaneously at the moment of new birth, even though the believer must grow into understanding it. And the clear evidence that it has occurred is that the Law moves from being merely an outward code to be obeyed to being a new law of our nature.

GOD'S WORK IN SANCTIFICATION

What does it mean that under the New Covenant God writes his Law on our hearts? There are two main aspects that we must understand.

First, it means that we no longer are under the Law as a covenant of *works* in obtaining right standing with God. Some Bible teachers and scholars make a distinction between our relationship to the Law when it comes to justification versus our sanctification. While they freely admit that the Law is not the means whereby we receive justification, they are quick to say that it is a powerful means of our obtaining sanctification. While there is much to learn about holiness in the Law, we must be careful not to posit the notion that justification is by grace while sanctification is by Law. The truth is, neither our justification nor our sanctification are obtained by observance of the Law. Both our justification and our sanctification are the result of God's work of grace in our lives.

Having said that, the second thing we learn about God's Law being written in our hearts is that it makes a life of *progressive* sanctification possible. That's because when we are regenerated, we *want* to do the things the Law requires (Romans 8:3-4). Not only is there a desire to live in accordance with the Law, we are empowered to do so. This occurs definitively at our regeneration and leads into a lifestyle which fulfills the Law.

I mentioned previously how, before I was converted, I regularly used the Lord's name in vain. But the moment I trusted Christ that desire to do so was totally gone. Even when I slipped up and used profanity after becoming a believer, I was deeply convicted and repented before God. Was this a result of my now trying to keep the Law? No; it was the law of Christ now at work in my heart which demonstrated that God's holy Law was now written there. This did not mean that I no longer sinned or always exhibited perfect righteousness, for I most certainly did not. But little by little, I began to live out the righteousness which was now written on the tablets of my heart. What was true of me *definitively* (that the Law was written on my heart) was now becoming evident *progressively* (by outward righteous behavior).

In our Lord's Sermon on the Mount, in the portion commonly known as the *'Antitheses'* (5:21-48), Jesus teaches his disciples what it means to have the Law written on their hearts by demonstrating its *true* meaning. We learn from this teaching that the real meaning of the Law was deeper than mere outward observance, although it will eventually be manifested in our outward behavior. The Jews of his day saw the Law as governing the outward *only*, thus ignoring the condition of their hearts. For example, Jesus taught that murder and adultery begin in the heart where anger and lust reside. The Jewish leaders thought they were not guilty of transgressing either of these commandments simply because they didn't literally murder or commit adultery. But Jesus teaches that murder and adultery begin first in the heart as thoughts of anger and lust long before they become actions.

This is why the New Covenant must be written on our hearts since that is where all true sin has its origins (Matthew 15:18-20). The Old Covenant merely restrained the behavior without really changing the heart. Under the New Covenant God writes the Law itself into our hearts so that we now obey from a transformed nature.

New Creatures with New Natures

The New Testament (based on the Old Testament) clearly teaches that those who have God's Law written on their hearts are nothing less than brand new creatures (II Corinthians 5:17). Years ago, I remember reading a translation of that verse which changed the word creature to *species*. That is certainly stronger than the word creature. A tadpole swimming in the creek, if it is given enough food and exposure to light, will eventually emerge as a frog. That's a new *creature* and in one sense it's a miracle. Yet the tadpole had it in him all along to become a frog if he remained in the right environment. But what if the tadpole became a canary? That's not a new creature—that's a new species!

The New Covenant therefore, takes the righteousness of the Law and writes it into the fabric of our hearts so that we now obey from a changed nature. Paul states it this way:

> *"For God has done what the law, weakened by the flesh, could not do. By sending his own Son in the likeness of sinful flesh and for sin, he condemned sin in the flesh, in order that the righteous requirement of the law might be fulfilled in us, who walk not according to the flesh but according to the Spirit."*

> *Romans 8:3-4*

The Law was weak, not in terms of being a revelation from God, but because of the weakness of human flesh. God condemned sin through the cross and gave the Church the Holy Spirit so that we could now live out what the Law demands. We don't do that by being under the Law as a covenant, but by being under a *New* Covenant which powerfully changes our natures. The righteousness of the Law is now fulfilled in us who are no longer in the flesh.

No wonder Paul told the Corinthians he didn't need a letter from them approving of his ministry since the Corinthians themselves were his letter ("And you show that you are a letter from Christ delivered by us, written not with ink but with the Spirit of the living God, not on tablets of stone but on tablets of human hearts" II Corinthians 3:3). The regeneration of these believers was ample proof that Paul was a minister of a "new covenant, not of the letter, but of the Spirit" (II Corinthians 3:6).

Chapter Seven

They Shall All Know Me

One of the most exciting aspects of marriage is the experiential knowledge each gains about their mate through time. When we first stand at the altar and pledge our vows, we have no idea what this vow really means. We know we are in love, but we have no way of knowing the depth of knowledge we will gain of our partner. That is one of the reasons the English Bible uses the word *know* when describing the physical intimacy which is reserved only for marriage ("Adam *knew* Eve and she conceived", Genesis 4:1). It is such a co-mingling of two individuals that it is said that Adam gained knowledge of Eve his wife.

One of the most powerful descriptions of the New Covenant God spoke through Jeremiah is the promise that all who are in this New Covenant relationship would have personal knowledge of God (Jeremiah 31:34). This is perhaps the grandest aspect of all the promises made. What was once limited to a few is now the privilege of all. Under the Old Covenant, only a few such as prophets and priests really knew the Lord. They heard God speak to them and received personal revelation of him, such as Abraham to whom God revealed Himself personally. However, such personal knowledge was not given to everyone but was reserved for those God chose. The common Israelite was not privy to this personal knowledge of God.

With the inauguration of the New Covenant, knowledge of God came to every covenant participant. Now, everyone who is under that covenant is promised personal knowledge of God: "For they shall all know me, from the least of them to the greatest," declares the Lord" (31:34b). That is not to say that the moment we are born again we have all the knowledge of God available to us. Not at all; we are meant to "grow in the grace and knowledge of our Lord and Savior Jesus Christ" (II Peter 3:18). But that knowledge begins the moment a person is born again. This knowledge is more than book knowledge but a personal knowledge of God himself.

Eternal Life…. Knowing God

What comes to mind when you hear the term eternal life? Most people, when they year the term or read it in Scripture, immediately think of it *quantitatively;* life without any end. They are right to do so since the term certainly implies that. Those who have received Jesus are given the gift of eternal life, which certainly means they will inherit life without end.

But it is interesting to note that the Bible, when defining eternal life, defines it not only *quantitatively* but *qualitatively.* Here is how Jesus described it at the beginning of his high priestly prayer: *"And this is eternal life, that they know you the only true God, and Jesus Christ whom you have sent"* (John 17:3).

Here, Jesus defines eternal life not essentially as a quantity of life but as a *quality* of life shaped by personal knowledge of God. Eternal life is beginning to know God in the present, leading to an eternity of knowing God. This knowledge of God does not begin in eternity but begins the very moment one partakes of the New Covenant. The Christian life, therefore, is being brought to knowledge of God through the new birth, leading to a life which increases in the knowledge of God. In other words, the moment we are born again, we are given knowledge of God which we then cultivate throughout the rest of our lives.

This knowledge of God must be personally gained through regeneration. While a person can be taught facts about God or may learn about God through reading the Bible or other books, only God can reveal Himself to a person so as to bring them into knowledge of himself.

Sometimes people refer to the knowledge of God given through the new birth as *intimate* knowledge rather than mere *intellectual* knowledge. When referring to Adam having sexual relations with Eve, Moses said, "Adam *knew* Eve his wife" (Genesis 4:1). Thus, the most intimate way that a man can know a woman is described as a gaining of knowledge. So, it is with our knowledge of God. It certainly includes the mind, but it goes much deeper than what we have learned from books or listening to sermons. It is *personal* knowledge of God gained through God revealing Himself to us.

Scripture makes it clear that God must always take the initiative in revealing Himself to us as Jesus Himself made clear in Matthew eleven:

> "At that time Jesus declared, "I thank you, Father, Lord of heaven
> and earth, that you have hidden these things from the wise and
> understanding and revealed them to little children; yes, Father,
> for such was your gracious will. All things have been handed over
> to me by my Father, and no one knows the Son except the Father,
> and no one knows the Father except the Son and anyone to whom
> the Son chooses to reveal him."
>
> *Matthew 11:25-27*

In these verses, Jesus praises God for choosing to reveal himself to those "little children" rather than to those who are "wise and understanding" in accordance with his eternal will (11:25). This is followed by the incredible statement that only the Father *really* knows the Son and the Son, the Father. While it is true there were those who have known both Father and Son throughout history, in the truest sense only the Father and Son *really* know each other. That's because only members of the Godhead could know each other at that level of intimacy. And not only does the Son *alone* know the Father in this fashion, He (the Son) chooses to whom he wishes to disclose the Father. This is the biblical doctrine of election, and it is found in every book of the Bible.

If I have come to know the Father, it is not because I have chosen to know him, but because the Son chose to reveal Him to me. I cannot boast in my knowledge as if it had anything to do with me (my upbringing, dedication, willingness, knowledge, wisdom, etc.). I have been given a revelation by the Son of the Father and that is the only reason I know Him. Of course, if I want that knowledge to grow and increase, I must cultivate it by using the means of grace: study, prayer, sharing my faith, fellowshipping with other believers, etc. But the initial knowledge, which I gain through the new birth is given to me by God the Son. There is no getting away from this fact.

This Knowledge Can't Be Taught

God spoke through Jeremiah that "*no longer shall each one teach his neighbor and each his brother, saying, 'Know the Lord,' for they shall all know me, from the least of them to the greatest, declares the Lord*" (Jer. 31:34). This knowledge of God is not a knowledge that can be taught through receiving instruction. Nor can it be learned from books. Based on what Jesus said in Matthew 11:27, it is a knowledge that comes from God alone. The promise God made through Jeremiah is that to those whom God has called, he has given personal knowledge of himself. This is true of everyone who partakes of the New Covenant.

Before our eyes are open in regeneration, we are ignorant of this knowledge of God. It is God alone who must reveal Himself to us; if he doesn't, we will remain in the dark. The apostle John in his first epistle affirms that this knowledge can't be learned through education. Speaking of those who would deceive believers, John says, "*you have been anointed by the Holy One, and you all have knowledge*" (I John 2:20). The knowledge John speaks of is the inherent ability to distinguish truth from error. This is not something that they must be taught, but is received from the Holy Spirit at regeneration. In fact, John goes on to say that they don't need anyone to teach them about this (distinguishing truth from error) because the Holy Spirit resides in them:

> "*I write these things to you about those who are trying to deceive you. But the anointing that you received from him abides in you, and you have no need that anyone should teach you. But as his anointing teaches you about everything, and is true, and is no lie—just as it has taught you, abide in him.*"

> *John 2:26-27*

Some have used this statement of John to assert that believers have no need of teaching. But John is not talking about *all* teaching in this statement but a special kind of teaching. Why would God include teachers as a part of the five-fold ministry, if the Body did not need teachers? (I Corinthians 12:28, Ephesians 4:11). In this passage, John is speaking about the specific knowledge the Spirit inherently gives regarding what is true and what is false. It is knowledge of spiritual reality and it is given to all believers once they receive the Holy Spirit.

ALL SHALL KNOW ME

God spoke through Jeremiah that under the New Covenant *all* would know him, from the *least of them to the greatest.* This is an amazing promise when viewed against the backdrop of the Old Testament. Let me explain.

As was stated previously, under the Old Covenant, only prophets, priests, and kings had the Spirit upon them. The prophets, for example, were men who were invited into the very presence and council of God; everyone else derived their knowledge of God through them. Under the New Covenant, though, no longer is this knowledge limited to these three specific offices, but all have been brought into the knowledge of God. It is true men like Paul were taken to the third heaven and given revelation of the divine purpose not given to others. Yet the knowledge of Jesus given to him at his new birth is given to us as well. He may have had special grace not given to others for ministry, but Paul was dependent on the Spirit of God to reveal Christ to him in the same way we are.

That is why the New Testament emphasizes the equality of all believers; we are all *brothers* and *sisters* sharing the same Father. While we have different gifts and abilities in ministry, we all share the same basic knowledge of God. Some might go on to cultivate a much deeper knowledge of God than others. But we all have come into the knowledge of God in the same way, through a revelation of the Father by the Son. That makes us equal in Christ, since we have all been given the same revelation. In the brotherhood there aren't some who know the Father and others who don't, but all have come to know him.

So often in the Church we define people by their ministry gifts and abilities rather than how they know the Father. We stand in awe of their gifts, which creates a wedge between us. But in the Church, the least and the greatest share the same birthright, no matter what gifts they have received.

The thing that defines the believer is that he or she knows the Father.

This is the amazing promise of the New Covenant. We all share this knowledge because we have been given eternal life which is, as Jesus said, to know God and Jesus Christ whom you have sent (John 17:3). What could be greater than to have come into the knowledge of God? While it certainly means we will live forever, it primarily refers to the fact that we have received a quality of life whereby we have come to know God. Since it is first a *quality* of life, there are certain things that should be evident in a believer's life when they have entered the domain of the knowledge of God. This will be described more fully in Chapter Ten.

CHAPTER EIGHT

NEW COVENANT CELEBRATION

To this day, one of the most enjoyable things I have the privilege of doing is leading a church through the Passover Seder meal. While the real Seder, the traditional meal Jews eat on the first night of Passover, can take up to three or four hours to go through, I usually give a shortened version in which I seek to reenact all of the events in the Upper Room when Jesus and his disciples sat down to eat that final Passover Seder. It is always insightful because many believers do not fully understand that the night the Lord's Supper was instituted, the disciples were celebrating the traditional Seder meal. *"This cup that is poured out for you is the new covenant in my blood,"* the Savior told his twelve closest friends at that last Passover Seder. He was referring to the third of four cups which would be taken that evening. That night, as Jesus took the third cup, He gave it new meaning. No longer would it represent deliverance from political bondage but a far greater deliverance from a far more pernicious tyrant: *sin*. The cup now portrayed deliverance from sin's bondage through the broken body and shed blood of the Lamb!

Interestingly, only Luke uses the article *'the'* in regards to the cup by which he instituted the Lord's Supper (Luke 23:20), no doubt a reference to the *third* cup commonly referred to as the Cup of Redemption. It was the most important of the four cups of wine which were taken intermittently throughout the Seder meal. That cup previously represented the Israelites' redemption from Egypt. He now revealed that it represented the *"new covenant in his blood."*

THE LORD'S SUPPER

The New Testament reveals the early disciples of Jesus celebrated the Lord's death by taking the two most important elements of the Seder, bread and wine, and, within the context of a meal, celebrated the New Covenant. This meal was referred to as the *love feast* (Jude 12) and the "Lord's Supper" (I Corinthians 11:20). This would be in keeping with the fact that early Semitic covenants were inaugurated by the sharing of a covenant meal. That it was a meal seems apparent from the simple fact that it was called the Lord's Supper rather than the Lord's Appetizer.

It appears the early church gathered around this table every Lord's Day:

> *"On the first day of the week, when we were gathered together to break bread, Paul talked with them, intending to depart on the next day, and he prolonged his speech until midnight."*

> *Acts 20:7*

Notice how Luke expressly says they did not gather together to listen to Paul. That is an amazing statement. If Paul was coming to a meeting of the church I would think the members would come in order to hear him. But Luke tells us they were gathered to break bread; the fact that Paul was speaking was secondary. Obviously, it was not the first time the Church did this, for it would appear that this was a regular practice. On the first day of each week (Sunday) they gathered together to celebrate the New Covenant by eating the covenant meal together. At that time, they also had the added blessing of hearing Paul speak.

This tradition of eating a meal to celebrate covenant extends back to the beginning of covenantal history. When Jacob cut a covenant with Laban after fleeing from him the Scripture says that they ate bread together before departing (Genesis 31:54). Moses and some of the elders of Israel went up into the presence of God and ate and drank in his presence after sprinkling both the people and book of the covenant with blood (Exodus 24:10-11). Of course, as we have already seen in this chapter, part of the Passover celebration included eating the Passover Lamb together (Exodus 12). As one author stated, "Eating with other people was a significant event in ancient days, for only parties who were at peace could dine together." The eating of the meal therefore was a symbol that those who were eating were reconciled to both God and one another.

The importance of recognizing the Lord's Supper as a meal celebrates the New Covenant and, as such, falls in line with the long history of covenant meals celebrated throughout the Old Testament. This fact (that the Lord's Supper is a meal) is demonstrated by Paul's rebuke of the Corinthian Church members for eating the Supper before the others had arrived and got drunk (I Corinthians 11:20). How could church members be filling their stomachs and getting drunk if the Supper consisted of only a piece of bread and a small thimble of wine? Only if the Lord's Supper were a full meal would this passage make sense.

Paul reminds the Corinthian Church: "as *often* as you eat this bread and drink the cup, you proclaim the Lord's death until he comes" (I Corinthians 11:26; italics mine). Today, it should read as *seldom* as you eat this bread and drink this cup, for few churches eat the Lord's Supper regularly. This robs God's people of one of the main means of keeping the New Covenant fresh in our minds and hearts.

THE CUP

Since the Lord spoke of instituting a *New* Covenant when he took the cup of Passover wine, it is imperative we properly understand the significance of the *cup*. For it is in understanding the cup that we understand the price our Lord paid to institute the New Covenant.

It is not exactly known when the Passover Seder was first attended by various cups of wine, but it is generally believed that these cups first appeared during the Babylonian Captivity. With the temple destroyed and no possible way to offer their Passover lambs, the Jews improvised by adding several new rituals to the Seder, including the taking of four cups of wine throughout the meal, each variously named (sanctification, deliverance, redemption, praise). If you count Elijah's cup, there are actually five cups throughout the evening but only Elijah (when he comes) was allowed to drink from his cup.

A cup of wine has two significant meanings throughout Scripture, the first being a symbol of judgment. For example, in Psalm 75 we read, "*For in the hand of the Lord there is a cup with foaming wine, well mixed, and he pours out from it, and all the wicked of the earth shall drain it to the dregs*" (Ps. 75:8). And in Revelation 16 we read, "*The great city was split into three parts, and the cities of the nations fell, and God remembered Babylon the great, to make her drain the cup of the wine of the fury of his wrath*" (Rev. 16:19).

We read in Scripture of a cup of *fury*, a cup of *judgment*, a cup of *trembling* and a cup of *horror* and *desolation*. We see throughout the Scriptures a cup is regularly used to signify God's unrelenting judgment against sin. Yet we also read in the Old Testament that a cup symbolizes salvation and redemption. The Psalmist declares in Ps. 116, "*I will take up the cup of salvation, and call upon the name of the Lord.*" The significance of that can be seen in the fact that during the Seder, there is a reciting of the *Hallel* consisting of Psalms 113-118. That meant that this portion of Psalm 116 would have been recited during the meal.

A *cup* symbolized both judgment and wrath on one hand, and redemption and salvation on the other. None of these references mentioned the Passover directly; nevertheless, the themes of judgment and salvation are woven together throughout the entire Seder. God poured out his wrath and fury on the Egyptians while saving and redeeming the Israelites who obeyed him by placing the blood of the lamb on the doorposts of their houses. The cup spoke of both realities.

As pointed out in the beginning of this chapter, Luke refers to the third cup as '*the*' cup rather than '*a*' cup (Luke 22:20). Judaism taught that the third cup actually had two names; the cup of *redemption* and the cup of *blessing.* Paul actually calls the communion cup the '*cup of 'blessing'* in I Corinthians 10:16. Jesus, when instituting the Lord's Supper, took the third cup and said, "This cup that is poured out for you is the *new covenant* in my blood"*(Luke 22:20,* italics mine). While not calling it the '*cup of redemption*,' he alluded to the fact that it represented the redemption which he would accomplish when he shed his blood for the sins of the world. This cup, which previously represented their redemption from Egypt, now represented their deliverance from a greater bondage—deliverance from the power of sin.

The night the Lord ate the Passover with his disciples, the twin themes of judgment and blessing were prevalent in his mind. He himself used the word *cup* twice that evening, the first being when he prayed in the Garden of Gethsemane:

"And when he came to the place, he said to them, "Pray that you may not enter into temptation." And he withdrew from them about a stone's throw, and knelt down and prayed, saying, "Father, if you are willing, remove this cup from me. Nevertheless, not my will, but yours, be done."

Luke 22:40-42, italics mine

As he entered Gethsemane that night he began to experience in his own Person the fury, judgment, and horror of bearing the sin of the world. Speaking of what the Lord Jesus experienced in the Garden, Norval Geldenhus said this:

"In every normal person there exists the urge to continue to live, accompanied by an aversion from suffering and death. Obviously, therefore, Jesus, who was completely Man and not subject to any blunting of His emotions or to any form of inward hardening, is infinitely more sensitive in his feeling or repugnance to unnatural things. It is impossible for Him, in his perfect humanity, not to experience a feeling of opposition to the idea of impending humiliation, suffering and death. And all this is made more intense through His knowledge that He is not only going to suffer and die, but that He will have to undergo this as the expiatory sacrifice for sin of guilty mankind. The judgment pronounced on sin is death—spiritual as well as physical. And spiritual death means being utterly forsaken by God. How dreadful then, must the idea have been to Christ, who from eternity lived in the most intimate and unbroken communion with His Father, that He would have to endure all this!"[8]

He goes on to say,

8 Geldenhus, N. (n.d.). The Gospel of Luke. In *New International Commentary on the New Testament.*

"No man will ever be capable of sounding the depths of what the Savior experienced in Gethsemane when the full reality of His suffering in soul and body, penetrated into his immaculate spirit."

Yet, in spite of the pain and horror and desolation he faced, there was nothing in the Savior which turned him back from taking it upon him. It is natural and right that, under the pressure of these circumstances, he should pray, "Father, if you are willing, remove this cup from me. Nevertheless, not my will, but yours, be done" (Lk. 22:42). The dreadfulness the Savior felt was so physically and emotionally intense, Luke records how he began to sweat great drops of blood. What accounts for this? It's called *hematidrosis* and it is a rare, but very real medical condition where one's sweat will contain blood. The sweat glands are surrounded by tiny blood vessels. These vessels can constrict and then dilate to the point of rupture where the blood will then effuse into the sweat glands. According to the experts, it is caused by extreme anguish. In the other Gospel accounts we read of Jesus' level of anguish in his words, "My soul is overwhelmed with sorrow to the point of death" (Matthew 26:38).

There is another mention of the cup in the Garden of Gethsemane. As the Savior was praying in the Garden, Judas came with the high priest's servant to arrest him. Peter drew a sword and cut off the high priest's servants' right ear. Remember how the Savior responded? "So Jesus said to Peter, 'Put your sword into its sheath; shall I not drink the cup that the Father has given me." (Jn. 18:11) What is the reason Jesus forbade his disciple from defending Him? After all, he could have called on twelve legions of angels to come to his defense. But he didn't because of his awareness that he must drink to the full the cup of the wrath of God. That *alone* is the reason Jesus forbade his disciples from defending him.

The New Testament uses the term *propitiation* to describe how Jesus bore the wrath of God for our sin. What is propitiation? "The word carries the basic idea of appeasement or satisfaction, specifically toward God. Propitiation is a two-part act that involves appeasing the wrath of an offended person and being reconciled to him." [9]

Some theologians are increasingly uncomfortable with this idea and deny that Jesus actually bore the wrath due to sinners in his own body on the cross. But looking at how the New Testament uses this term (Romans 3:25, Hebrews 2:17, I John 2:2) makes it undeniable that the writers used this term to convey that Jesus bore our wrath by his death.

The Supper: Looking Ahead

The New Testament teaches that the Lord's Supper has two significant meanings. First, "as often as you eat this bread and drink the cup, you proclaim the Lord's death until he comes" (I Corinthians 11:26). Every time we take it together, we are proclaiming that the Lord has died. That is the only reason that we are a New Covenant community—the Lord has purchased us with his blood.

But there is something else proclaimed when we eat the Lord's Supper that is prophetic in nature: We are eating it as a foreshadowing of that time when we will eat it with the Lamb at his Supper. Jesus Himself alluded to this the night he was betrayed when he said, *"I have earnestly desired to eat this Passover with you before I suffer. For I tell you I will not eat it until it is fulfilled in the kingdom of God"* (Luke 22:15). Jesus looked forward to the time when the foreshadowing which the Lord's Supper represented would give way to the reality: the 'Marriage Supper of the Lamb' as John reveals in the Revelation (Revelation 19:7). Every time we take the Lord's Supper

---

9 G. (2017, January 04). What is propitiation? Retrieved March 20, 2017, from https://www.gotquestions.org/propitiation.html

on earth therefore we are looking forward to the time when we will eat it together at the Lord's appearing.

God, in his grace, has given us a visible expression of that great day in the Lord's Supper. When we eat and drink it on earth it serves as a reenactment of the day when we will sit down with the Lamb in a renewed heaven and earth and eat together. The kingdom has already come in the Person of Jesus which is why we now celebrate the Supper. But it is not yet here in its consummative form. For that we wait and while we wait, we eat and drink to both remind ourselves that we have been redeemed by the Lord's death and await the kingdom in its fullness in the new Jerusalem.

CHAPTER NINE

NEW COVENANT FREEDOM

The passionate cry of a dying William Wallace, the leader of the Scottish resistance aimed at independence from England, was "Freedom!" That last scene of Braveheart, where his torturers attempt to get him to recant and fail, solicits instead his warrior-like cry for *"freedom"* and made him a national hero. The brutal nature of his death and his unswerving commitment to freedom gained him a permanent place among the greatest Britons in history.

Jesus Christ purchased our freedom through much agony and suffering as well; far more, in fact, than William Wallace endured. Freedom, in a word, isn't free! It cost God his greatest gift—giving up the Son of his love to excruciating pain and anguish at Calvary so as to inaugurate a New Covenant, whereby guaranteeing freedom to those who receive it. By far, the most powerful thing about the New Covenant is the promise made by God to write his laws on our hearts and inward parts.

In the light of these powerful promises, how then should we live? The key word that should describe a New Covenant believer is the word *freedom*. New Covenant believers should be the freest people on the planet since these promises offer a freedom no other religion can offer. Such freedom is not the result of lowering standards but the result of having been freed from the need to please God in ourselves. The believer is free from both sin and the Law as God writes his law into the very fabric of our hearts.

In this chapter, we will examine the different ways we are free under the New Covenant. To the degree that we are not experiencing these, to that degree we do not adequately understand and believe the New Covenant. Freedom is inherent to life under the New Covenant. The saddest thing on earth is a Christian who is not living in the full measure of this freedom. Considering all that God in Christ accomplished to inaugurate a New Covenant, we must consider it sin for a believer to be living a life of bondage, fear, unbelief, and compromise. Nevertheless, many believers live this way, even while claiming to be under the New Covenant. Few indeed are the churches where this freedom is both practiced and preached. Unlike the Lord who, upon raising Lazarus from the dead, told those standing around to *"unbind him, and let him go"* (John 11:44), many churches keep people bound in their grave-clothes. This is sad indeed.

Here are the three areas of freedom we should be experiencing under the New Covenant:

FREEDOM FROM THE LAW (ROMANS 7:1-4)

Since the Law was a *"guardian until Christ came in order that we might be justified by faith"* (Galatians 3:24), that means the believer is no longer under the Law when it comes to his or her standing before God. While that doesn't mean we should live lawless lives, it does mean that we don't derive our righteousness from our own perfect performance under the Law. Rather, our righteousness is obtained by faith in God who declares us righteous through the perfect work of His Son. This is the Gospel way of being made righteous.

Indeed, many believers start their Christian life this way, but find themselves in churches where the Gospel way of achieving righteousness is not properly taught. The result is they live constantly under condemnation, trying to earn righteousness through observance of the Law rather than by faith. That is the way I started my early Christian life. I was taught that I was forgiven when I believed in Jesus, but after initially being forgiven, I was on probation to see how I would do. Each week, I worked really hard at walking in obedience. Nevertheless, by the end of the week, I felt like I fell short no matter how hard I tried. All I could do was to come to church and repent of my having fallen short, pledging to do better next week. And without failure, at the end of each week I found myself again confessing my sin and pledging to do better the following week.

It was only after repeated failures that I eventually realized that I was living by the principle of *law* rather than that of *faith*. Jesus had already declared me righteous through his perfect work. It was faith *alone* that reaches out to accept this free gift of righteousness. Paul describes this life of faith in God's righteous gift this way in the Galatian letter:

> *"For through the law I died to the law, so that I might live to God. I have been crucified with Christ. It is no longer I who live, but Christ who lives in me. And the life I now live in the flesh I live by faith in the Son of God, who loved me and gave himself for me."*

Galatians 2:19-20

In the Roman epistle, Paul uses the analogy of a married woman to demonstrate what freedom from the Law means (Romans 7:1-6). If a woman is married and is joined to another she is called an adulteress, but if her husband dies she is free to be joined to another without being called an adulteress. Paul, in verse four, applies this to the body of Christ: "*Likewise, my brothers, you also have died to the law through the body of Christ, so that you may belong to another, to him who has been raised from the dead, in order that we may bear fruit for God.*" As long as we are alive we are under the law but if we die, the Law no longer has jurisdiction over us. And the fact is, if we are "in Christ Jesus", we have already died to the Law through the death of Christ to whom we were joined. That death terminated our relationship to the Law and joined us to Another—to him who was raised from the dead. Now we can bear fruit for God.

This is in keeping with what Paul says in the balance of the seventh chapter of Romans. There, the apostle teaches how the Law worked to stir up sin (7:9). The Law only brought fresh reminders of sin as it worked on Paul's conscience. But that was its purpose to begin with— to magnify sin so that it became even more sinful. The Law has done its work when we become aware of how sinful we are. Then, we are prepared to receive the gift of righteousness, which is to be received only by faith.

Since we are no longer under the Law we are free from the condemnation that results in our failure to obey it. Not that we are to live lawless lives, for we are now under the law of Christ. But we are no longer under law as a principle by which we achieve acceptance with God; our acceptance with God is based on the fact he has justified us through his blood rather than, on the basis of, our perfect obedience (Romans 5:9). And this is the basis by which we continue to find our acceptance with God. We are not justified initially by faith and then, on the basis of our performance. Rather, even after our initial acceptance by God through faith, we continue to find our acceptance with God through faith rather than our performance.

Legalism is the dreaded enemy of the Gospel because it teaches that though we are initially justified by faith and not by Law, we can only continue to be justified on the basis of our performance. Though I was initially taught that forgiveness was by faith, I lived under the fear that my performance was not up to par. But once I learned the truth of the Gospel and God's justifying grace, I learned my performance was never the basis for my acceptance but ever and always Jesus Christ and the gift of his free grace. I could come to the *"throne of grace"* to find *"mercy and grace to help in time of need"* (Hebrews 4:16). It is always a throne of grace we are invited to which means that the basis of our coming is never in what we have done, but in what God did in Christ.

Whenever I read that phrase *"throne of grace"*, I immediately think of the story of Esther. Ester took her life in her hands since no one could approach the king's throne unless summoned by the king. But as Esther waited for the king's approval, the king held out the golden scepter to her which meant she was accepted and could come.

In the same way, if we approach the throne of God, on the basis of our own goodness or performance, there is nothing but certain death awaiting us. But since it is a throne of grace we may always come at all times, knowing God will accept us. That's because the Law is never the basis of our coming but God's grace. The demands of the Law have been satisfied and therefore we never have to wonder if we will be accepted. No; the writer of Hebrews tells us that we come with *"confidence to enter the holy places by the blood of Jesus, by the new and living way that he opened for us through the curtain, that is, through his flesh"* (Hebrews 10:19). Jesus made a new way for guilty sinners to come into the presence of God. As long as we come by faith in the blood of Jesus, we can be assured that we will be accepted for Jesus' sake.

FREEDOM FROM CONDEMNATION (ROMANS 8:1)

Because we are free from the Law, we are also free from the condemnation that breaking the Law brings. Paul states succinctly that *"there is therefore now no condemnation to those who are in Christ Jesus"* (Romans 8:1). This is a powerful statement, especially considering it comes after his thorough description of the life of failure and bondage to sin that living under the Law brings (Romans 7:14-25). We have already seen the connection between the Law and transgression: *"For the law brings wrath, but where there is no law there is no transgression"* (Romans 4:15). Whenever we try to live under Law, failure is the inevitable result. And when we fail to keep it, we are justifiably condemned.

But the good news of the Gospel is that Jesus *kept* the Law for sinners, having exhausted in himself the condemnation we deserve for our failure to keep it. Therefore, there is no condemnation left since God condemned his Son in our stead. Sinners are under condemnation, but those for whom Christ died, God no longer condemns us, but pardons us freely.

Condemnation is a legal term which is a sentence from a judge. Outside of Christ, there is nothing but condemnation, for we have broken the Law and must bear the penalty. But now that the demands of the Law have been met through the perfect righteous life of the Lord Jesus and his atoning death, there remains no more condemnation. And not only that, God did what the Law could not do: *"By sending his own Son in the likeness of sinful flesh and for sin, he condemned sin in the flesh, in order that the righteous requirement of the law might be fulfilled in us, who walk not according to the flesh but according to the Spirit"* (8:3). That means that while he condemned sin in the flesh, he gave the Spirit to those who belonged to him so that by living in the Spirit, they might live righteous lives.

On a practical level, this means that we no longer need to carry around a low-grade guilt due to condemnation. Sadly, many of God's children still do. So many are accustomed to living with a sense of the Lord's disfavor, they have mistaken this condemning voice as the voice of the Holy Spirit. But when we realize that the Father's justice has been satisfied and that the perfect righteousness of Christ has been put into our account, we can live with a sense of the Lord's favor instead of fear and judgment. The apostle John said it best: *"There is no fear in love, but perfect love casts out fear. For fear is associated with punishment, and whoever fears has not been perfected in love"* (I John 4:18). With the threat of punishment removed, we can now live in unbroken fellowship with the Lord.

It is important to distinguish between the convicting power of the Holy Spirit when he is dealing with a particular issue in our lives and the condemnation we often carry due to our feeling we fall short of the mark. This has been called *false* guilt; a feeling of guilt without knowing what we are guilty of. At those times, we must learn how to lift up the *"shield of faith"* to *"extinguish all the flaming darts of the evil one"* (Ephesians 6:16). The believer is pictured here as being constantly assaulted by incoming missiles, which surely includes the enemy's continual voice of condemnation. The only way to defeat these attacks is by believing the Gospel; we are righteous in God's sight because of the perfect work of his Son. When we are established by faith in the truth of the Gospel, no missile can penetrate that shield of faith.

Therefore, the only way a believer can resist condemnation is by understanding what it means to be "in Christ." The believer now shares the history of the Son of God; his history is *our* history. Sometimes when I am teaching on being *'in Christ,'* I use an illustration I borrowed from one of Watchman Nee's books. Holding up a piece of paper in one hand and a book in the other, I drop the book on the floor. I then ask the congregation what happened to the paper when I dropped the book on the floor. Of course, the answer is nothing. The book and the paper have two separate histories and what happens to one does not affect the other. But then I slip the piece of paper in the book and drop the book on the floor. What then happens to the paper? It goes to the floor with the book since the paper is now *in* the book. They no longer have separate histories but now share the same history.

The believer now has no condemnation because he or she is *in* Christ Jesus (Romans 8:1). We share the history of the Son of God who, according to the writer of Hebrews, *"always lives to make intercession for them"* (Hebrews 7:25). This means more than that he is praying for us; it suggests that his very presence before the Father as our righteous Advocate guarantees our acceptance by him! (I John 2:1).

When I am teaching this in churches, I often point out that the Lord Jesus was the first one to test the efficacy of the blood. How? Because of the fact that He bore the sin of the entire world in his own Person. How then was he able to enter back into the presence of God since he bore our sin? The writer of Hebrews supplies the answer:

> *"But when Christ appeared as a high priest of the good things that have come, then through the greater and more perfect tent (not made with hands, that is, not of this creation) he entered once for all into the holy places, not by means of the blood of goats and calves but by means of his own blood, thus securing an eternal redemption."*
>
> *Hebrews 9:11-12, bold italics mine*

Jesus Himself had to enter *by means of his own blood.* Therefore, if Jesus is able to enter the presence of the Father by means of his own blood though bearing the sin of the world, what could ever keep us from entering as well?

FREEDOM FROM SIN (ROMANS 6:7,11,14)

The Apostle Paul, while teaching the Roman church the meaning of justification, states clearly that "sin will have no dominion over you, since you are not under law but under grace" (6:14). The believer has been "set free from sin" through the redeeming work of Calvary. Indeed, it is one of the clearest evidences that one has been regenerated; that their entire attitude towards sin has now changed.

Some have taken Paul's words that sin will no longer have dominion over us to teach a doctrine of sinless perfection—that human beings, through grace, can come to the place where they no longer sin. This is not at all what the apostle is teaching here. Other Scriptures make it clear that such perfection is impossible in this life (I John 1:8). Rather, he is teaching that the dominion of sin has definitely been broken so that sanctification is now possible. In justification, we are delivered from the penalty of sin but in sanctification we are delivered from the *power* of sin (one day we will be delivered forever from the *presence* of sin when we are glorified). Deliverance from the power of sin does not mean sinlessness, but it does mean its power is progressively waning in our lives, making a life of obedience now possible (I John 3:4-10). For example, a person living in sexual immorality who is converted cannot remain in that illicit relationship. For as the Apostle John says, *"We know that everyone who has been born of God does not keep on sinning, but he who was born of God protects him, and the evil one does not touch him"* (I John 5:18). A person who is born of God does not need to be told they are sinning for there is planted in them a consciousness of sin upon being regenerated.

I once spoke with a couple seeking to become members of the church where I served as a teaching pastor. I noticed on their application that the man and the woman had different last names, so I was compelled to ask them about it. They freely admitted without any hesitation that they were living together as well as being sexually active, though unmarried. Armed with this knowledge, I took them through a brief Bible study on what Scripture had to say about sexual immorality and more importantly, God's attitude towards it. When I was done the man looked at me and said, "None of this ever occurred to us." I knew by this answer that neither of them were Christians. While I told them why I could not accept them as members of our church, I did plead with them to repent of their sin and come to faith in Jesus Christ.

Some might take issue with my readiness to conclude this man and woman were not saved, positing instead that they might be infants in need of discipleship. But in saying that, we minimize or ignore completely the transformative power of regeneration. While I certainly believe in discipleship, it can never take the place of real, transformative conversion. Though I was sexually active before conversion, after my conversion, I knew I could no longer remain in sexual sin, even though no one had told me that. Impure thoughts now convicted me, whereas previously my conscience didn't bother me in the least. This was not the result of things I learned in discipleship, but having received the new life of the New Covenant.

We will deal with this more in the next chapter on New Covenant holiness. For now, suffice it to say that the New Covenant introduces human beings to a level of freedom which no human religion or philosophy provides. The Son of God said it best: "He who the Son sets free is free indeed" (John 8:36).

CHAPTER TEN

NEW COVENANT HOLINESS

One of the most frequent accusations hurled at those who preach the grace of the Gospel is that if they are not careful, they will encourage people to sin. We've heard it before—preach grace and people will distort it and live careless lives, justifying their sin. The supposed answer to this is to give them just enough law to balance out grace. In other words, if you preach grace alone you are encouraging people to sin.

The technical term for this is *antinomianism, which* literally means "against law." Apparently, those of us who have had this accusation aimed at us are in good company; the apostle Paul himself was accused of the same thing (Romans 6:1). In fact, it is safe to say that unless you have had this said about your preaching, you are not preaching the grace of the Gospel.

Nevertheless, the idea that preaching grace alone will promote sin is ludicrous. For the grace the New Covenant offers doesn't merely cover sin, but removes it entirely. While it is true that both justification and sanctification were accomplished for us by the redemptive work of Christ, both being something that occurs *outside* of us (I Corinthians 6:11), yet there is a continuing work of sanctification in the believer's life whereby he or she experiences power over sin. The power of the New Covenant is the promise we can walk in a new depth of practical holiness.

Holiness is not optional in the life of the believer. The writer of Hebrews tells his readers to *"strive for peace with everyone, and for the holiness without which no one will see the Lord"* (Hebrews 12:14). Paul speaks of our "bringing holiness to completion in the fear of God" (II Corinthians 7:1). There is a serious neglect of this theme in the Church today. Many believers are given false assurance that they will see the Lord, despite what these Scriptures say.

It is true that we are *"justified by his blood"* and that *"we have confidence to enter the holy places by the blood of Jesus, by the new and living way that he opened for us through the curtain, that is, through his flesh"* (Hebrews 10:19). Nevertheless, when we are justified and come to the Father through the new and living way he opened for us, we are totally *transformed*. Holiness becomes our normal, day-to-day deportment. As James writes in his epistle, faith must be accompanied by works or else it is dead (James 2:14-26). In other words, a truly justified man or woman will give evidence of their justification by a transformed life of holy living.

The New Covenant promises not only that God will forgive our iniquity, but that he will put his law within us and write it upon our hearts (Jeremiah 31:33). We saw in chapter six that this occurs at the moment of regeneration. The prophet Ezekiel described what God does when he regenerates a person: *"I will give you a new heart, and a new spirit I will put within you. And I will remove the heart of stone from your flesh and give you a heart of flesh"* (Ezekiel 36:26). In that moment, the person's hard, unbending heart is replaced with a soft, responsive heart. And respond he does, first, by believing upon the Lord Jesus Christ unto salvation and secondly, by beginning to live a holy life, separated unto God. Evangelicals tend to stress the first, leaving the second as optional. But according to the promises of the New Covenant, holiness is not optional but evidence God has written his laws upon our hearts.

HOLINESS AND THE NEW BIRTH

The title of this chapter is *New Covenant Holiness*. That is important because it is only as the New Covenant is fully embraced that holiness, which God both demands and promises, can be achieved. In other words, a holiness based on the Old Covenant is powerless and will always produce failure.

In the Old Testament, God required that his people be holy in every aspect of their lives (Leviticus 11:44). Israel was a people who were set apart for the Lord from their inception. Yet, the long history of the nation is the record of failure when it comes to living holy lives. Even after receiving the Law and pledging that "all the words that the Lord has spoken we will do" (Exodus 19:8), they rejected God by making a golden calf as a symbol of worship (Exodus 32). We have already seen in chapter two the long history of their failure to keep the covenant.

This demonstrates the powerlessness of the Old Covenant and the Law. It was a perfect Law and the covenant under which it was ratified was good, but we are "carnal, sold under flesh" (Romans 7). Unless we receive a changed nature, we cannot keep the Law and are doomed to perpetually break the covenant. Therefore, it is grace and grace *alone* which allows us to be holy. Grace is not merely forgiveness for breaking the Law; it is empowerment to live righteous lives in the here and now. The only way true holiness can be achieved in Christ is by living in and by the grace of God.

This is New Covenant holiness—God actually writing his laws on our hearts and minds so that we manifest his nature. Because the Law is engraved on stone tablets and not on the tablets of human hearts, holiness is unattainable. In the other great prophecy describing the New Covenant found in Ezekiel, God describes how both justification and sanctification are achieved (Ezekiel 36:25-27). Justification is first described in the promise that God will "sprinkle clean water on you and you shall be clean from all your uncleanness" (36:25). This is the cleansing which occurs when a person is justified. But the promise goes on to describe the creation of a new nature as well: "And I will give you a new heart, and a new spirit I will put within you. And I will remove the heart of stone from your flesh and give you a heart of flesh. And I will put my Spirit within you, and cause you to walk in my statutes and be careful to obey my rules (36:26-27). The first depicted in verse 25 is clearly a picture of justification whereby God sprinkles us clean by the blood of Jesus so that we are cleansed from all of our sins (I Peter 1:2). The second is the result of the first: *God puts his Spirit in us so that we can live holy lives.*

Both of these occur at the moment of regeneration when God creates a new nature in a person by removing the heart of stone and replacing it with a heart of flesh (vs. 26). The result is that he now causes us to "walk in my statutes and be careful to obey my rules" (vs. 27). We should pay careful attention to the fact that the end result of God's regenerating work is that the believer now walks in his statutes, living a life of obedience and walking in holiness. This righteous living, according to the apostle John, is the evidence that one is truly born-again (I John 3:1-10). Yet it is the result of regeneration, not the cause of it. In other words, when a person is born again, the verifiable result of this miracle is that the believer begins to live a righteous, holy life. According to John, this is the way that the children of God and the children of the devil are to be distinguished.

Many Christian leaders today are reticent to teach this biblical truth, that those who claim to belong to Christ will live righteous, holy lives. In fact, in order to get around it, many posit the notion of the 'carnal' Christian, which is loosely based on Paul's words to the Corinthians (I Corinthians 3:1-3). According to this belief, a carnal Christian is a person who has been born again, yet still lives a life totally directed by the flesh. Such a person is considered to be a Christian, albeit a *carnal* one. But this is at variance with what Scripture teaches. While it is certainly true that believers may, at times, think and act in a fleshly way, no *true* believer can live a life completely dictated by the flesh. That's because the believer is no longer living in the flesh, but in the Spirit if they have been born again (Romans 8:9). It's not a matter of whether, at times, the Christian acts carnally; at times, they can and often do. But that is a far cry from the idea that a person can be a Christian and be *totally* dominated by the flesh. This idea has allowed people who are not really regenerate to be deceived into thinking they are true Christians.

While every believer will still manifest some fleshly traits on their way to developing practical holiness, there will be ever increasing elements of a holy life visible as a person grows in Christ. Still, the first dawnings of holy living should be evident at the new birth. Earlier in this book, I told how before I was converted, I used to curse like a sailor. Yet, the moment the life of God entered me, I immediately stopped. I didn't take a course or attend a seminar on how to stop cursing; once the life of God entered, I knew instinctively that my lips were not my own and that that my words must edify and build others up. The point I am making is that this came naturally to me so that the moment I was regenerated, so I did not have to try to stop cursing. Since what Jesus said is true, that from the "abundance of the heart the mouth speaks", once my heart was transformed, I no longer used such language.

God had done what He promised to do under the New Covenant: To put his laws into our minds and write them on our hearts (Hebrews 8:10). I had experienced what God promised through Ezekiel when he promised he would "give you a new heart, and a new spirit I will put within you. And I will remove the heart of stone from your flesh and give you a heart of flesh. And I will put my Spirit within you, and cause you to walk in my statutes and be careful to obey my rules" (Ezekiel 36:26-27).

Holiness and Grace

Looking carefully at verse twenty-seven of Ezekiel thirty-six, we note the phrase, "cause you to walk in my statutes." It holds the key to New Covenant holiness. As stated in a previous chapter, under the New Covenant, the *conditions of the old are now the promises of the new*. In the Old Testament, walking in his statutes was the basis of blessing. For example, he promised to bless the agricultural efforts of the Israelites *only* if they walked carefully in his statutes (Leviticus 26:3). Many other blessings are promised to the Israelites under the Old Covenant, but they are all conditioned on the obedience of the people.

But when we come to the New Testament and look for the conditions of blessing, we discover there aren't any! All we find is the promise of what God would do for his people by giving them a "new heart and a new spirit" and removing the "heart of stone", replacing it with a "heart of flesh. And He promised to give the Spirit as an inward possession, thus securing our obedience so that we can receive the blessing. The end result is summed up best by the Apostle Paul in the Philippian letter: *"It is God who is at work in you!"* (Philippians 2:13).

The critical difference between the Old Covenant way of achieving holiness and that of the New Covenant is that the Old Covenant was outward, while New Covenant holiness begins *inwardly,* working itself outward. Most religions emphasize the practice of certain performances and the carrying out of rituals as the way of achieving holiness. They are based on the principle of *works;* the attaining of righteousness by the keeping of outward forms and the performing of certain rituals. But in the Gospel, righteousness is given as a gift, which frees us from fruitless dead works to serve the living God (Hebrews 9:13-14). What are dead works the writer of Hebrews refers to? They are useless attempts at keeping the Law as a means of working off guilt.

They are dead because they are performed by dead sinners and are therefore not the result of faith in Jesus. For whenever we attempt to work off guilt through our perfect obedience we are bound to fail, since no amount of works can cleanse our conscience.

I had to learn that the hard way in my early days of learning to follow Jesus. One of the things I struggled with the most in those initial years of being a disciple was my prayer life. I knew that prayer was vital to a fruitful life, but I struggled being devoted to it. It would seem that for a while I was disciplined, but would eventually slip back to an undisciplined prayer life. It was during that time that I was given a biography of a great English prayer warrior and I read it, hoping it would inspire me to a greater prayer life. This great man would rise at 3: 00 a.m., each morning to spend time with the Lord. As I read, I felt guilty I didn't do the same and determined God was calling me to follow his example. So, I purposed to rise at the same time each day to set aside several hours to seek the Lord. For a while I was successful and was able to keep my pledge, but eventually I fell back to my previous state. And as a result, I felt very guilty about my failure to follow through on my previous commitment.

It was while I was dealing with the guilt of having failed to keep my pledge I felt the Holy Spirit whisper to me, "Why don't you confess to me that your heart is cold and ask me to give you the grace of a praying heart?" As I heard this, I realized what I had done. When I read the biography of the great prayer warrior, I felt guilty that I didn't pray as much as he did. Instead of dealing with the root problem (my cold heart), I started an elaborate works program to work off guilt. Thus, it was a *dead* work since anything done to try to deal with guilt without dealing with the real problem (sin) can never cleanse our conscience. In light of the great promises in God's Word to answer prayer, prayerlessness is not merely a problem, but sin. What I needed first was not discipline, but to be honest before God about my true condition—I had a cold heart. That was my sin, and the only way to deal with sin is to confess it and receive God's cleansing. Then, and only then, could I receive grace to help in time of need (Hebrews 4:16).

And that is exactly what happened. After confessing my sin of prayerlessness, I received the grace of a praying heart. It was no chore afterwards to be disciplined in prayer since God had forgiven me for my coldness and given me the desire to commune with him more. Now I pray, not to work off guilt but because I desire to have fellowship with my Lord. The Lord truly poured out on me a spirit of grace and of supplication (Zechariah 12:10, NASB). It was not duty which now drove me, but a genuine desire to fellowship with God.

Holiness and Faith

We are already made holy in Christ when we are set apart to God by the new birth as the Apostle Paul states clearly (I Corinthians 6:11). That doesn't mean that we are as holy in practice as we can be. But by the new birth, God separates us from the world unto himself. Notice how the apostle uses the past tense to describe our having been set apart in Christ: you "*were* washed, you *were* sanctified, you *were* justified in the name of the Lord Jesus Christ and by the Spirit of our God."

Paul, when testifying to King Agrippa, states how Jesus told him on the Damascus Road he was sending him to the Gentiles to "open their eyes so they may turn from darkness to light and from the power of Satan to God, that by faith in Me they may receive forgiveness of sins and a share among those who are sanctified" (Acts 26: 18). Notice how Paul says it is by *faith* that the Gentiles would receive both forgiveness of sins as well as a "share among those who are sanctified." We are accustomed to associating faith with justification alone, but here Paul associates it with our sanctification as well. That's because it takes faith not only to receive justification, but also to receive sanctification. Many have been taught that while we are justified by faith, we are sanctified by our works. But these words of Jesus to the apostle of the Gentiles make it clear that sanctification requires faith every bit as much as our justification does.

The writer of Hebrews says the believer has been "sanctified through the offering of the body of Jesus Christ once and for all" (Hebrews 10:10). Again, the writer of Hebrews states it succinctly: "For by one offering He has perfected forever those who are sanctified" (10:14). Both of these statements posit sanctification as a finished work. Notice how the writer stresses Jesus offered up his body "once and for all." It is as a person believes the truth about this finished work that he or she finds power to live out the practical outworking of their having been sanctified. To attempt to live out sanctification without faith in the prevenient sanctifying work of the Son is to live a life of frustration.

This does not negate James' word that "faith without works is dead" (James 2:17). Those who believe they are sanctified in Christ will have works to prove it. While justification is *monergestic* (God's work alone), sanctification is *synergistic*—dependent on both human effort and divine accomplishment. Sadly, most believers emphasize the human side of the equation when it comes to sanctification; the things we must *do* to achieve holiness in this life. But without the solid Scriptural emphasis that the believer is already sanctified by the eternal work of the Son of God who offered himself up at Calvary by which he has "perfected forever those who are sanctified", there will be no power to actually walk a holy life in this world. Little wonder that so many are frustrated when it comes to achieving holiness in this life.

So, the starting place for living a holy life is to first believe that his death was sufficient to perfect us forever. We *are* sanctified by the perfect work of Jesus Christ. Faith in that truth deadens sin in us and gives us the desire to live holy lives in this world. Don't get me wrong: true faith in the reality which Jesus accomplished through his death will produce a holy life. But it is only in looking away from ourselves to what Jesus did that this holiness is possible. Dr. Martin Lloyd Jones stated it this way:

"We can put it this way, the man who has faith is the man who is no longer looking at himself and no longer looking to himself. He no longer looks at anything he once was. He does not look at what he is now. He does not even look at what he hopes to be as the result of his own efforts. He looks entirely to the Lord Jesus Christ and His finished work, and rests on that alone. He has ceased to say, "Ah yes, I used to commit terrible sins, but I have done this and that." He stops saying that. If he goes on saying that, he has not got faith. Faith speaks in an entirely different manner and makes a man say, "Yes I have sinned grievously, I have lived a life of sin, yet I know that I am a child of God because I am not resting on any righteousness of my own; my righteousness is in Jesus Christ and God has put that to my account."[10]

HOLINESS AND HUMILITY

The Apostle John in his first epistle says, *"If we say we have no sin, we deceive ourselves, and the truth is not in us. If we confess our sins, he is faithful and just to forgive us our sins and to cleanse us from all unrighteousness"* (I John 1:8-9). These words of John instruct us that the only way to achieve practical holiness is to live in the light about our true condition. Legalistic holiness focuses largely on our behavior, while the holiness which grace achieves freely admits its failures. And it is encouraged to do so by the conviction that no matter what we confess, he will cleanse it by the power of the blood of Christ.

This encourages us to be honest about our lives, which is a key to attaining true holiness of life. Jesus told a story that illustrates how God responds to the humility which is honest before God. It is found in Luke's Gospel:

"He also told this parable to some who trusted in themselves that they were righteous, and treated others with contempt: "Two men went up into the temple to pray, one a Pharisee and the other a tax collector. The Pharisee, standing by himself, prayed thus: 'God, I thank you that I am not like other men, extortioners, unjust, adulterers, or even like this tax collector. I fast twice

10 https://www.goodreads.com/quotes/803945-we-can-put-it-this-way-the-man-who-has

a week; I give tithes of all that I get.' But the tax collector, standing far off, would not even lift up his eyes to heaven, but beat his breast, saying, 'God, be merciful to me, a sinner!' I tell you, this man went down to his house justified, rather than the other. For everyone who exalts himself will be humbled, but the one who humbles himself will be exalted." Luke 18:9-14

Although Jesus said that the tax collector went home *justified,* this illustrates the pathway to sanctification as well. The Pharisee was blind to his own sin, focused entirely on the good things he did: he "fasted twice a week and gave tithes of all." But the tax collector was fully aware of his failure to live a holy life and could not even lift up his eyes to heaven. Instead, he beat his breast asking repeatedly, "God, be merciful to me, a sinner." Jesus said that he went home justified. But he also went home *sanctified.* What I mean by that is that this was the proper foundation for a life of holiness. That's because holiness of life begins and ends with *humility*.

If the true saint is one who wants to rid his life of sin, then humility is essential to having a proper assessment of our lives. It is only those who humble themselves before the light of God that bring "holiness to completion in the fear of God" (2 Corinthians 7:1). The first aspect of living a holy life, therefore, is that we are quick to confess whatever the light of God reveals. Yet, it is the knowledge that he is "faithful and just to forgive us our sin and cleanse us from all unrighteousness" that encourages us to be scrupulously honest.

The Psalmist perhaps said it best: "If you, O Lord, should mark iniquities, O Lord, who could stand? But with you there is forgiveness, that you may be feared" (Psalms 130:3-4). A proper knowledge that God forgives us our sins always leads us to a proper fear of him. Far from giving us an excuse to sin, the knowledge of his mercies makes us quite sensitive that we are walking carefully before him. This is the true motivation to live a holy life. This is, in fact, what New Covenant holiness is all about.

CHAPTER ELEVEN

NEW COVENANT COMMUNITY

Listening to most evangelistic messages preached today, there is very little ever said about the Church. The appeal usually is to individuals to recognize their need of a relationship with God, and the call goes out for those same individuals to respond. The Church, if it's mentioned at all, is an afterthought or an addendum: "Oh, and by the way, once you accept Jesus, attend the church of your choice." If the Church is mentioned at all, it is only in passing at best. It would seem it is clearly not that important.

Yet, this is a far cry from what is normative in the New Testament. When Peter preached the Gospel for the first time on the Day of Pentecost, three thousand souls responded and received his word. And Luke is careful to mention that these three thousand who believed were *added* to the Church: "Those who believed what Peter said were baptized and added to the church that day—about 3,000 in all" (Acts 2:41, NLT). They weren't serving Jesus somewhere in the stratosphere but were actually added to the visible assembly and began to partake of the devoted life described in Acts 2:42. This was more than an occasional practice but a *lifestyle* of devotion to certain practices the entire community engaged in. The fact that the three thousand had repented and now believed the Gospel was evident by one thing: that they had left one community and now entered another.

This experience of community for the Jerusalem believers was a by-product of the Judaism they had known from birth. When a million Jews stood at Mount Sinai and heard the voice of the living God inaugurating the covenant with them, a covenant community was born. God didn't merely save individuals out of Egypt but an entire community, bringing them into covenant with himself.

Because of that, the Jewish people grew up with a sense of belonging to a community. This can be seen by the fact that no Jewish prayer ever begins with the word *'I'* but *'we.'* When Jesus taught his disciples to pray what we commonly call the 'Lord's Prayer', he told them to begin by addressing God as *Our* Father. We are to come to him as part of a community rather than as individuals. Even today, Easterners in various parts of the world identify themselves first in terms of the community they belong to, rather than their individuality. Ask them who they are and they will respond by telling you the people group they are a part of.

Not so in the West. Asked who we are, we commonly answer by describing who we are *individually;* what we *do* and things of that nature. It is one of the evidences that radical individuality has replaced biblical community in the West. But the Bible was written in an Eastern culture, where community is still the way that most people identify themselves.

The promise God gave in the New Covenant was that of the emergence of a new community: "I will be their God, and they shall be my *people*" (Jeremiah 31:33). It is a corporate community which now partakes of the New Covenant. It was God's intention to bring a community into covenant mercies through Jesus Christ. In this chapter, we will explore all that this means.

The 'Let Us' Patch

I sometimes refer to Hebrews 10:19-25 as the "*let us*" patch (i.e. *lettuce patch*) when I have taught it in the past. Three times the writer of Hebrews uses the phrase "*let us*" when exhorting believers to respond to the call to enter the presence of God through Jesus Christ. The writer summarizes certain realities he has firmly established throughout the book. In verses 19-21, the efficacy of the blood as the basis for the believer's confidence, the new and living way this has opened up for those who come to God through Jesus, and the greatness of his present role as our faithful High Priest over the house of God are all clearly taught. Now, on the basis of all that he has said about Jesus and his great work, he gives three strong exhortations the people of God must apply to their lives.

Two things should be noted as we look at these two words ("*let us*") which form the basis for this exhortation. First, the word *let* is a grace word. To let something happen is to allow something to function according to its inherent desire or purpose. It is the opposite of the Law with its commanding, "thou shalt". The gracious "*let us*" implies that we want to anyway—we just need to '*let it*' happen. It is what has been called a 'gracious' exhortation. When our hearts are warmed by grace, we are enabled to *let* certain things happen.

The second word *us* serves as a reminder that this is a community wide exhortation. It is not merely for individuals, but for all the people of God. We in the West are so accustomed to thinking of spiritual development as only a personal matter, we almost never think of ourselves as belonging to a community. But this, and the myriad of other exhortations in God's Word, teaches that the whole community must apply the benefits of redemption. Three times this gracious call to the community of the redeemed is issued, each one inviting us to experience the fullness of salvation. This is what lies at the heart of New Covenant community.

The first is an exhortation to draw near as the people of God to the throne of grace (10:22). It is the call to the community of the redeemed to live in the reality of his presence. We are to do this with a "true heart, in full assurance of faith." 'True' in this sentence is akin to *sincere,* a heart totally honest and sincere regarding what it is seeking. We are to come in sincerity, totally convinced that what we are seeking we shall find. We can do so since we have our "hearts sprinkled clean from an evil conscience and our bodies washed with pure water." The first is a reference to the fact that the atoning blood is sufficient to deal with our evil conscience, while the second is the reminder that in our baptism, we "put off the old man" and have "put on the new man." These two things (blood and water) correspond to the two pieces of furniture in the Outer Court of the Tabernacle: the Brazen Altar where the blood of innocent victims was sprinkled, and the Laver, where the priests washed before entering the sanctuary.

The second *"let us"* exhortation is aimed at promoting trust in God throughout the community: "Let us hold fast the confession of our hope without wavering, for he who promised is faithful" (10:23). The phrase the *"confession of our hope"* is the confession of the great hope the community has through the Gospel in the glory of God. Paul states it this way in the Roman epistle: *"We rejoice in hope of the glory of God"* (Romans 5:2). When believers gathered together, they would often make this confession in the assembly.

The third use of the phrase *"let us"* has to do with the purpose for which we gather together—to stir up each other to "love and good works" (Hebrews 10:24). We are to come together not merely to receive, but to give what we have to the saints. We can only do this by not neglecting to *"meet together, as is the habit of some, but encouraging one another, and all the more as you see the Day drawing near"* (10:25). The Greek word translated by the phrase "meet together" in the text is the word *episynagoœgeœ* which is to meet together formally as in a synagogue. It is to be gathered together for worship and to hear the Word of God taught.

Apparently, some saints saw little need for such gatherings in the first century even as many do not see a need today. Perhaps they used the same excuses then as we do today—"it's too formal and we don't get anything out of it." Or perhaps they felt it more profitable to just meet with saints sporadically rather than gather in formal settings for worship and Gospel instruction. Whatever the reason, the Word of God clearly spells out that we need these formal gatherings more and more as we see the Day drawing near. As far as the writer of Hebrews is concerned, gathering in these formal settings is an important part of being a New Covenant community. While entering community is primarily more than simply attending Church meetings, it certainly includes it. For as we shall see in the next chapter, the community is sustained by a continual hearing of the New Covenant through the medium of preaching.

No More Shame

It is helpful to recognize how the New Covenant fosters deep and intimate relationships among God's people. It is a byproduct of the fact that the New Covenant deals with that which is the main culprit in relational superficiality— *shame*. Until we realize how the work of Christ profoundly deals with our shame, we will not risk the transparency needed to move behind superficiality. Many today seem satisfied with such relationships.

Reading the Genesis account of creation, we learn that man and woman dwelt in utter transparency both before God and each other before the Fall: "The man and his wife were both naked and were not ashamed" (Genesis 2:25). They were able to look upon each as they really were without any feeling of shame. But that ideal situation didn't last long. After being deceived by the serpent in the Garden who convinced them that eating of the fruit of the tree of the knowledge of good and evil would make them more like their Creator, they were now ashamed of their nakedness (Genesis 3:7). What was once a natural and affirming state (their nakedness) now caused sheer terror. The first couple experienced what was previously unknown: a sense that they were flawed and, therefore, less than they should be. So, what did they do? They immediately sought to remedy the situation by sewing fig leaves on and covering their nakedness. In other words, shame made them hide from one another by seeking their own way of covering themselves.

And that is what the human race has been doing this since the Fall—hiding behind our outward coverings so as to engage others without allowing them to see who we really are, all the while living in terror that we might be found out. What are these coverings? Usually, they are religious works of various sorts, giving the appearance that we are respectable, while hiding our true selves from the penetrating eyes of others. This allows us not only to hide our true selves, but also to achieve our sense of self-worth by comparing ourselves to others so as to feel better about ourselves.

Thank God, he did not leave us without hope, but planned a way for community to be restored. The Gospel was preached in the Garden to our first fallen parents, restoring them both to God and to each other. Stripping them of their fig leaves, he killed animals, clothing them with the skins (Genesis 3:21). No more could the human race deal with shame by hiding behind our religious works (fig leaves). Rather, we must be clothed with garments the Lord God has prepared for us.

Only the Gospel has the power to deal with the shame of our fallenness. It is the great, grand, merry news that the Father has provided us with 'garments of righteousness'—not the skins of animals but the perfect righteousness of God obtained through the death of his Son. This is a perfect righteousness which satisfies all claims to justice. It is *justifying grace*, which means not only we are now "just as if I had never sinned" but also "just as if I had already obeyed." He died, not only to deliver us from the penalty of our sin, but he also lived a perfect life so his perfect record could be applied to us as well. A person can be forgiven of a sinful act, yet still bear the shame of their misdeed. But in justification, we are not only forgiven ('just as if I had never sinned'), we are also treated as we had never sinned ('just as if I had always obeyed').

Since we are totally accepted by the blood of Jesus, we no longer need to cling to our fig leaves, because we are now clothed with God's own righteousness. Nor do we have to hide from others, since our shame has been swallowed up by a full and complete atonement of sin. We can therefore be real about our weaknesses and failures, because our identity is no longer tied to our performance. This frees us to have intimate relationships of love, trust, and accountability. Whereas this invitation to intimacy was previously a scary thing, it is now something we not only want, but also thoroughly enjoy.

ENJOYING INTIMACY

What should these intimate relationships look like which are now made possible under the New Covenant? In Psalm 122, we are given a picture of three levels of relationships available to us as members of the body of Christ: *superficial, rubbing,* and *bonding.* Let me explain what each represents.

Superficial level of relationships can be seen in the opening words of the Psalm: "*I was glad when they said to me, 'Let us go to the house of the Lord!' Our feet have been standing within your gates, O Jerusalem!*" (122:1-2). This is the congregational level of relationships. This level should not be undermined, for standing in the assembly with other saints is the beginning level of relationships. We all entered church life at this level. In most churches, though, people rarely go beyond this level and remain superficial when it comes to their relationships. I once knew a couple who came to church faithfully but would rush out at the end of the service before we ever got a chance to meet them. It became a joke between one of the other pastors and me as to who would meet them first.

God has called us beyond the superficial level of relationships to the next, which is best described by the word *rubbing*. The Psalmist describes it in these words: *"Jerusalem—built as a city that is bound firmly together, to which the tribes go up"* (Psalm 122:3-4). He is describing the swelling crowds as the tribes made their way from their various towns and villages up to Jerusalem at the Passover. It has been said that the crowd of pilgrims quadrupled at that time so that you couldn't avoid rubbing up against others. The counterpart to this is to engage God's people on a level which allows for friction and rubbing. Just as in marriage rubbing and friction are impossible to avoid in order to go deeper, so also in attaining the full measure of blessing of relationships in the body of Christ. Sadly, many people bail out at the first hint of conflict, and thus never experience the full blessing of intimate relationship with the body of Christ.

But for those who are willing to work through the inevitable conflict that comes through ever deepening relationships the final stage is reached: *bonding* best described by the Psalmist's words, *"Pray for the peace of Jerusalem! May they be secure who love you! Peace be within your walls and security within your towers! For my brothers and companions' sake I will say, Peace be within you! For the sake of the house of the Lord our God, I will seek your good"* (122:6-9). These are relationships where we truly are seeking the good of others. There is a bonding that takes place which goes beyond mere friendships. It is the kind of selfless, intimate relationship we were meant to enjoy in the body of Christ.

Only as we partake of the grace promised under the New Covenant can we ever hope to move beyond the superficial level of relationships through rubbing into bonding. That's because it is only where the full measure of blessing the New Covenant promises is received and enjoyed that we can be sure to gain ever-increasing intimacy with the saints.

Chapter Twelve

New Covenant Preaching

When I first started in the ministry, I was a street preacher. I was the guy you crossed the street to avoid. I would roam about Miami Beach with my two best friends, fellow-Jews who had powerfully met the Messiah, looking for crowds to whom we could preach the Gospel. We often went to synagogues and waited for them to come out on the Sabbath. As they filed out of the synagogue, we would lift up our voices and begin to proclaim Jesus of Nazareth as the Jewish Messiah. On a good evening, we would be hit by umbrellas and cursed out. I remember many times going back to our house thanking God that I was allowed to suffer for his Name.

Looking back, I realize now that much of our preaching in those days was ill advised. But it was there, almost forty-five years ago, that I first felt a call to pursue what is the most wonderful thing a person can be occupied with—preaching the Gospel. For over four decades I have had the privilege of preaching the Word. It is, to be honest, both the most wonderful and most difficult thing I have ever done. I can relate to other preachers who have said that even after many years of preaching, they still haven't felt like they preached a good sermon. Perhaps I have come close, but still I don't feel like I've hit the mark.

The last two chapters of this book deal with the relationship of the local church to the New Covenant. The final chapter addresses the subtle (and not so subtle) legalism which often replaces the Gospel when the New Covenant is not fully embraced. This chapter addresses one of the safeguards God has given us against such legalism: *preaching*. One of the ways God has created for his people to know and grow in the New Covenant is for God's people to sit under preaching which is both rooted in as well as aimed at illuminating the New Covenant. Churches that have New Covenant preachers are richly blessed.

There is a growing belief among many today that preaching is no longer needed in the Church. After all (we are told), we are living in a time when people are resistant to objective truth claims and should therefore look for better ways of communicating so that moderns will hear. Ours is a postmodern culture and people resent having truth claims forced on them. Instead, we should move towards more 'dialogical' ways of communicating the message. We should *share* and *talk* to people, which is much less intrusive than preaching.

I have no problem with the idea of 'dialoging' or 'sharing' the Gospel, believing they are all valid ways of communicating the Gospel. I make the point in this chapter though that preaching is still God's ordained way of making the Gospel known. As long as the Church remains on earth, God will use preaching as the most important way for the Gospel to advance. That is not to say that he won't use these other means as well; he will and we should therefore use them. But he has given a special place to preaching that is different from these others. Paul defends the idea that preaching is necessary when he tells the Roman church that "faith comes from hearing, and hearing through the word of Christ" (Romans 10:17). Contrary to popular opinion, this passage is not talking about personally hearing God's voice speaking to you. Rather, it is Paul's defense of why preaching is necessary. It is the only way that men and women can have faith in the Gospel:

> *"How then will they call on him in whom they have not believed? And how are they to believe in him of whom they have never heard? And how are they to hear without someone preaching? And how are they to preach unless they are sent? As it is written, "How beautiful are the feet of those who preach the good news."*

> *Romans 10:14-15*

As long as faith is necessary for our salvation, so also is preaching. This is true not only in making the Gospel known to those who have never heard, but in building up the saints as well. But such preaching is only a blessing when it is New Covenant preaching; proclamation solidly built on the truth of the grace of God as revealed in the New Covenant. As we will see in the final chapter, there is a type of preaching which is really modeled after the Old Testament and cannot, therefore, be called 'New Covenant' preaching at all.

WHY WE STILL NEED TEACHERS

We need to begin by first addressing something often misunderstood and which leads, at times, to undermining the importance of preaching. When God spoke to Jeremiah in the great prophecy about the New Covenant, he promised that: *"No longer shall each one teach his neighbor and each his brother, saying, 'Know the Lord,' for they shall all know me, from the least of them to the greatest, declares the Lord"* (Jeremiah 31:34).

This promise, that as a result of the New Covenant there would no longer be a need for teaching, is often used to undermine the need for preaching and teaching in the Church. Since (according to this view) every person now possesses direct knowledge of God, there is no longer a need for teaching them to *"know the Lord"*. But as we examine this prophecy more carefully, we find that Jeremiah is not saying that there will be no need of teaching; rather, that a certain *kind* of teaching will no longer be necessary. He is referring to the kind of teaching given in the Old Testament which instructs people to "know the Lord." Under that covenant, the knowledge of God could only be known externally.

All of that changed when the New Covenant was inaugurated. Now, the knowledge of God is not given as a result of listening to teaching but by an operation of the Spirit of God working deep within human hearts. This is the kind of teaching that is no longer needed, since those under the New Covenant have already gained a knowledge of God, which is both personal and inward and is only given to men and women through the new birth.

Shouldn't that do away with the need for teaching in the Church, since every man and woman under the New Covenant already knows the Lord? On the surface, one might think so. But then we are faced with the question, "Why then does God appoint teachers in the body of Christ as one of the five ministry gifts by which the saints are equipped (I Corinthians 12:28, Ephesians 4:11)? If God appointed teachers along with other ministry gifts to the Church, there must still be a need for them. While there is no longer a need for the kind of teaching that tells people how to know the Lord, there is still a need for teachers to clearly explain the Gospel so that men and women can put their faith in Christ, as in the case of Apollos at Corinth (Acts 18:27).

There is still a need for teachers, even though believers have gained personal knowledge of God through the new birth. They affirm from Scripture what we have learned inwardly by the Spirit. Teaching has the wonderful way of giving God's people a rationale for their faith. Many times, when I have taught in a church, someone will come and say, "I've always felt this was true, but didn't have the words to express it." I always know that I have done my job when I hear that. The Spirit had already been teaching that person—my words simply gave expression to what the Spirit already revealed. This is wonderfully uplifting to the saints and gives them a scriptural basis for their faith.

PREACHING THE NEW COVENANT TO SINNERS

We have already seen that God still uses preaching as the main means of advancing his kingdom on earth, both by preaching the Gospel to sinners and building up the Church. Not all preaching promises to accomplish that but only that which can clearly be characterized as 'New Covenant' preaching. What exactly is meant by the term 'New Covenant' preaching?

First of all, New Covenant preaching is preaching which understands that it is grace and grace alone which can change men and women, and that that grace comes through faith in the Gospel. Therefore, it is rooted in the belief that only God by His Spirit can change lives. As we have seen from the great prophecy of Jeremiah, God must 'put his laws into their minds, and write them on their hearts' (Hebrews 8:10). So, the one who preaches the New Covenant properly is one who is totally dependent on God if anything is to happen. Pastor John Piper said it this way: "The new covenant is not a mere possibility; it is a new creation. It is something not merely that God proposes, but something that he accomplishes."[11]

I once heard of a seminary professor who taught homiletics (the science of preaching) who took his students to a cemetery and told them to begin preaching to the tombstones. The students hesitated, not sure what exactly their professor was trying to teach them. Finally, he explained it. When they were preaching the Gospel to sinners they were actually preaching to dead

11 Sermon: The New Covenant and the New Covenant People. (1993). *People*, (February 7).

men and women who have no chance of coming alive unless God raises them. It is exactly what God was saying to the prophet Ezekiel when he set him down in a valley full of dry bones and told him to prophesy (preach the word). The words themselves had no power. So how did they come together and begin to live? It is because of what God said: "Thus says the Lord God to these bones: Behold, I will cause breath to enter you, and you shall live" (Ezekiel 37:5). But this only began to happen when Ezekiel obeyed the word and began prophesying. This is a clear example of how God uses the preached word to accomplish his redemptive purposes.

Ezekiel is a powerful example of how God uses preaching to affect change. New Covenant preaching is preaching based on the belief that just as God was at work to bring the bones together and give them breath when Ezekiel spoke the word, so also, he works through New Covenant preaching. Going back to what Pastor John Piper said, it doesn't merely propose; it accomplishes. In other words, preaching doesn't create the possibility of setting up an event—preaching is the event!

I have seen this happen many times over the years. I remember a woman who was an atheist who began to attend our church. We gave her literature to read and answered her questions as she studied. One Sunday night, I was attending a small group at a friend's house, and she was there. As we chatted before the meeting started, she began to share what she had experienced listening to the preaching that morning. What was clear as she talked is that she had been regenerated as she listened to the message. As far as I recall, the message that morning was not about how to become a Christian, and there was no altar call given. Still, this woman was saved. It was a vivid example that: "faith comes by hearing and hearing by the word of Christ" (Romans 10:17). She believed as she heard and was born from above.

This is why New Covenant preachers need to be people of prayer. There is a mystery to preaching that is difficult to explain. Certainly, it is required of preachers that they are accurate, but they must also be men of prayer who are constantly asking for conversions through their ministry. New Covenant preaching is best carried out in an atmosphere of faith that believes that God will be at work as the message is preached in the conversion of sinners.

PREACHING THE NEW COVENANT TO SAINTS

We have seen that an important part of church life is for the saints to sit under the preaching and teaching of the New Covenant. It is a powerful means of keeping the Gospel front and center in the lives of the saints. There is a grace released whenever the preaching of the New Covenant occurs. John Piper tells of a time when he was preaching a series in his church on the nature and attributes of God. Little did he know that, while he taught this series, a couple was devastated to learn their young child had been sexually molested. At some point in the series, they told their pastor what sustained them during that difficult time was the greatness of God they had learned through the preached word.

That demonstrates how God uses preaching in the life of the people of God to encourage and sustain them, especially in time of need. I have personally experienced times when I was in despair or was unaware of a besetting sin which had taken hold of my life, which was exposed while sitting under Gospel preaching. The light of God's Word exposed it, and I needed no other counseling. A simple word from God delivered me from despair and helped me go on.

Martyn Lloyd Jones, one of England's greatest preachers of the twentieth century, in his classic book on preaching, *Preaching and Preachers*[12] talks about how properly preaching the Gospel in the Church cuts down on the counseling load for pastoral ministry. His main reason for saying that was that true Gospel preaching answers people's problems so that there is little

---

12 Lloyd-Jones, M. (1971). *Preaching and preachers*. London: Hodder and Stoughton.

need for them to talk to a pastor to help them with their problem. That was the case in the example just given from John Piper's ministry. The young couple that discovered their child was being molested did not seek out their pastor for pastoral counseling about this matter, though we could hardly blame them if they had. They felt no need to, as their need was met through the ministry of the Word. That is exactly what Lloyd-Jones meant when he said that a biblical preaching ministry cuts down on the counseling load.

I have had this happen in my own ministry as well. Some people have felt the need to apologize for not needing my specific counsel about a situation. Instead, they felt that God helped them as they listened to the Word of God. I always thank them for telling me that and was always quick to tell them there was no need to apologize: I had done my job if they didn't need me.

This is the power of the ministry of the Word in the Church today. An expository ministry which preaches through all of Scripture is a powerful means of making sure that the things Paul told Timothy are derived from Scripture (II Timothy 3:16-17) and are, in fact, being produced in the lives of the saints. First of all, preaching the New Covenant means that the saints will be well established in the great doctrines of the faith (II Timothy 3:16). They will also be reproved by such sermons, because the Word of God is the ultimate source of reproof. *'Reprove'* is translated from the Greek word *'elegcho,'* which means to 'convict, refute or confute (prove a person or an assertion to be wrong). Sermons based on God's Word also bring correction—they not only show us what is wrong, they also demonstrate how to correct it. Finally, if we are serious about living the Christian life, sermons that teach Scripture will help to train the saints to live godly lives in this present world.

PREACHING GOOD NEWS

It goes without saying that New Covenant preaching is rooted in the declaration of God's good news. It is the great, grand, merry news that God, in Christ, reconciled the world to himself and has now committed to the Church the *'ministry of reconciliation'* (II Corinthians 5:18). It is the announcement of what God has done and, therefore, is monergistic—driven by God's work alone.

The fact that it is good news and not good advice defines its nature as a preached word as, D.A. Carson reminds us:

> *"Because the gospel is news, good news... it is to be announced; that is what one does with news. The essential heraldic element in preaching is bound up with the fact that the core message is not a code of ethics to be debated, still less a list of aphorisms to be admired and pondered, and certainly not a systematic theology to be outlined and schematized. Though it properly grounds ethics, aphorisms, and systematics, it is none of these three: it is news, good news, and therefore must be publicly announced."*[13]

This is why the Gospel needs to be preached. You don't preach advice; you give it. But news means that something has happened, and the only thing left is to announce it. It's already done, and people just need to hear about it. That is why Gospel messengers are called 'preachers.' They don't tell people how to live, but declare what God has done in Christ so that others might believe (Romans 10:17). The only acceptable way to respond to the message is by believing it. Faith can only come as men and women hear the good news. That is why we will always need New Covenant preachers in the Church. The Gospel is the proclamation of the good news of what God did in Jesus Christ. We will always need to hear it, because left to ourselves, we will always preach a different message to our hearts.

This is besides the fact that many of the people we regularly preach to do not understand the Gospel. Why? Because there is very little New Covenant preaching in the Church today. Much of the preaching focuses on advising

---

13 Daily Keller, Wisdom from Tim Keller 365 Days a Year, D.A. Carson, http://dailykeller.com/good-news-not-good-advice/.

people how to live rather than announcing good news. Despite the fact that we use New Covenant language, much of our preaching is Old Covenant in nature. And so are many of our practices. More about that in the final chapter.

CHAPTER THIRTEEN

OLD COVENANT CHURCHES

After my powerful conversion in 1971, I came with great hunger to my first church, eager to learn how to follow Jesus and share him with others. Having recently read through the book of Acts, I expected to find all of the things which characterized the early church; passionate preaching of grace, transparent relationships, miraculous signs, and contagious community.

Instead, I was told that to become a member, I must first sign a card pledging not to engage in certain activities such as drinking and smoking and some others (I think one was bowling). I found it strange that I had to sign a card pledging not to do what I no longer wanted to do anyway, since God had so changed my nature through the power of the New Covenant. Nevertheless, I signed it because I really wanted to be a part of the church.

I immediately began attending our Tuesday night and Sunday morning services. Our pastor was incredibly gifted at inflicting guilt, and he did it with great skill and careful attention to detail. He repeatedly told us each week how we had failed to pray enough, read our Bibles enough, witness enough; do just about anything required of us. When the sermon ended, we would rush the altar and repent for our failures, pledging to do better in the coming week. Nevertheless, we were back the following week, repenting of the same things once again and summing up all our resolve to give the Christian life a better try in the week to follow.

I am not writing this to any way disparage my first pastor. He loved the Lord and really desired to encourage us to give our all to Jesus. But looking back four decades later, I realize our church was caught in a Christianized version of the Old Covenant. We talked about the New Covenant and how Jesus had forgiven us, but we lived in the belief that blessings were totally dependent on how well we performed. We never would have said that but occasionally it slipped out. One of the first times I preached in our church, I really felt my words were powerless. When I asked my pastor after the message why it seemed I did not connect with the people, he asked me how many hours of prayer I had engaged in before I preached. When I told him I had *only* prayed four hours for the message, he said that that was the reason. The inference was clear: If I had put in six to eight hours of prayer, I would have had a more powerful message.

Needless to say, I lived the majority of my beginning years in the faith with a profound sense of failure. No matter how hard I tried, I never felt like I measured up. I couldn't, since I was trying to live the Christian life under an Old Covenant mindset.

Old Covenant or New Covenant Preaching

Just as the Law given under the Old Covenant was the means of revealing the Israelites' failures and thus bringing condemnation, so also was much of the preaching I sat under. Its aim was to condemn us by showing us our failures. Sadly, once we were condemned, we were never brought to Christ who alone could rectify our situation. Instead, we were taught how to be reliant on our own works. We were made to feel bad, in the hope that our guilt would prod us to love and good deeds.

This is clearly an Old Covenant mindset and always ends in failure. For, as the writer of Hebrews says, ("the law made nothing perfect); but on the other hand, a better hope is introduced, through which we draw near to God" (Hebrews 7:19). The law can convict the conscience, but it is powerless to deal with our failure. For that, we need to be introduced to a better hope—a hope which deals completely and thoroughly with our sin and guilt. And that hope is only found in the Gospel.

Unfortunately, this was not just a problem our church had, but is systemic throughout the worldwide body of Christ. It is the result of believing that the Gospel is the message that only gets you *in*—once you are in, you need something else to keep you. Drop into the majority of the churches any given Sunday and you are apt to hear a lot more about what we need to do for God than what God did for us. I am not suggesting that there is no place for the saints to be taught regarding biblical responsibilities. The Bible is full of imperatives; various commands regarding the behavior of the saints. But unless imperatives are preceded by indicatives, (clear declarations of the good news of what God did in Christ), they can easily become little more than a moral code. And since no one perfectly obeys, we end up feeling like failures, carrying around a low-grade guilt.

A pastor I know was once preaching in Romania with a well-known evangelist. Being well known, the evangelist was preaching at the larger, evening rallies while my friend had the smaller, daytime sessions. After two days, though, the leaders of the conference came to my friend and told him they wanted him to do all of the meetings the following day. Puzzled, my friend declined, but they were persistent. When he asked them why, they simply said, *"He told us what we must do for God; you told us what God did for us."*

Sadly, most people in most churches today hear a steady diet of what they must do for God and are therefore strangers to New Covenant preaching. Is it little wonder that they live the entirety of their lives feeling like they constantly fail God? Since they are basing their standing with God at any time upon their perfect performance, they are doomed to fail. And the result is that they are made to acutely feel that failure from the pulpit.

Over the years, I have had the privilege of preaching through the book of Ephesians in several churches. In my thinking, the way Ephesians is laid out perfectly reflects what New Covenant preaching should look like. For the first three chapters (arguably the clearest exposition of the Christian life ever written) the apostle does not mention a single imperative (command) but gives a series of indicatives—clear statements of how the entire triune God contributed to our salvation. Words are piled upon words in breathless wonder as the apostle expounds the work of the triune God in making us his own. It is only after establishing that our salvation is totally God-initiated does he then, in chapters four through six, describe our fitting response to the grace of the Gospel. Yes, faith always *responds* to the Gospel and produces works. Without such works, as James points out, faith is dead and useless (James 2:17).

Much of the preaching I grew up under had this reversed. We were first told about what we had to do, and then what God's response was when we were faithful to perform. At best, we were prisoners who, after being released from our jail term, were put on probation to see how we would act. This type of Old Covenant preaching always warned us of what might happen if, for whatever reason, we let our guard down and slipped up. I remember, as a new believer sitting in a theater watching a perfectly good and wholesome movie, fearing the entire time that I might miss the Rapture if it should come at that moment. Needless to say, it ruined the movie for me. But that is what Old Covenant preaching does; it makes us fearful and unbelieving that God can keep us by his power.

Someone reading this might misunderstand me to be saying there is never a place for rebuke or correction in the preaching of the New Covenant. The truth is, both (grace and warnings) are found in the New Testament, often side by side. The writer of Hebrews, for example, in the passage we looked at previously in chapter ten (Hebrews 10:19-25) graciously invites us into God's presence based on the finished work of Christ. And he graciously extends an invitation ("let us") to enter the community of the redeemed where we are to "consider how to stir up one another to love and good works." But if we read on, these gracious invitations are followed by a stern warning (10:26-31) of what will follow if we refuse to receive the grace of God. Grace is free, but there are serious consequences if we fall short of it. So, there is a place for stern warning alongside gracious invitation in preaching the New Covenant.

Many churches, which claim to be serious about teaching people how to live out the New Covenant, are living under the Old. There are many evidences of this, but these two are most apparent. First, there is the focus on getting people to the altar in order to receive from God. Secondly, there is the subtle tendency to view pastors as priests who mediate God to the people they pastor.

COME TO THE ALTAR

Just as there was an altar in the Old Testament sanctuary, I grew up believing there was one in the Church as well. It was the place where God really met people: In the front of the sanctuary, at the altar, sinners and saints must come to transact with God.

Let me say that I have no fundamental problem with saints coming forward to receive prayer in the front of a sanctuary. But like other traditions, this one has unconsciously fostered the idea that people must come to a certain spot in order to receive from God. We don't mean to, but that is the impression we give, since we are always inviting people to come up to the altar.

Even the fact that we call it the altar means we are associating it with the Old Covenant altar, although that is not what the Old Covenant altar was. It (the Old Covenant altar) served as a place both of memorial and of sacrifice. The Patriarchs (Abraham, Isaac and Jacob) built altars in response to the revelation of God they received. In the Old Testament Tabernacle, the first piece of furniture you came to when you entered is the Brazen Altar; the large, altar where Israel brought their sacrifices to atone for sin. The priests would serve at that altar, offering the sacrifices for the people. The sin offering was the offering mostly offered on this altar because sin was our greatest problem. That was why a bull was used for the sin offering, because it was the largest animal to deal with the greatest problem.

How did we get from the Old Testament Brazen Altar to the altar at the front of the church building where we must come to meet God? It is commonly attributed to nineteenth century evangelist Charles Finney who perfected the altar call and used it in evangelism to call sinners to repentance. Its original name was the 'mourner's bench' and served as the place he would call people to identify those under religious conviction. Originally, no one thought just coming to the front of the church saved anyone. Eventually, coming forward was considered akin to salvation. Sometime in church history, leaders began to invite Christians to come to the altar as well and there receive from God. Christian teachers soon began to associate this with the Old Testament burnt offering. The burnt offering was viewed as the typical sacrifice by which the Israelite offered himself up to God in repentance and consecration.

What is interesting, though, is that the two types of sacrifices offered on the altar have nothing to do with our response to God, but are actually types of the sacrifice of the Messiah on behalf of sinners. The sin offering portrays Christ as the Sin-Bearer who alone bore in his own body our sins (I

Peter 2:24). The burnt offering portrays Christ offering himself perfectly to God on our behalf. Both of these offerings are types of the atonement Jesus provided for guilty sinners.

I once sought to make this point when I was speaking to the pastoral staff of a church I had recently come to, where I served as senior pastor. One of the staff had said he felt it was important that we have frequent altar calls in which we called people to total surrender to God. I replied by asking, "Why, since nobody can (totally surrender)?" I pointed out that God apparently knew we couldn't, since he sent us One who totally surrendered on our behalf. I went on to point out that the altar we really need to be calling people to is the cross, where our glorious Savior gave up his lifeblood and thereby put away sin, once for all (Hebrews 9:26). It is faith in the work accomplished at Calvary that provides the grace to 'give up our lives' for the Savior. This is the real altar to which we should be calling people.

MY PASTOR, MY PRIEST

Another way many churches are more closely aligned to the Old Covenant than the New is in the attitude many of God's people exhibit towards leaders. Rather than receiving them as gifts from God for the building up of their faith, many saints view pastors and leaders as *priests*—mediators between God and themselves. If a pastor or leader is present in a meeting, they are usually asked to lead in prayer. There is a subtle belief (rarely expressed) that pastors and leaders have a more direct line to the Father than the average saint. Somehow, if you can get a pastor to pray for you, you have a better chance of getting your prayer answered.

This is really not just a recent phenomenon, but has plagued the Church from its inception. By the early second century, many churches had moved away from being governed by a plurality of male elders, which is the biblical norm, to a single bishop who ruled over a church. It was only a matter of time before that bishop was endued with priestly power. This gave birth to the clergy/laity distinction; that bishops and pastors are in the ministry while others are not, which is a far cry from the biblical norm that all of God's people are priests, having direct access to the throne and ministering in the unique graces each has been given (I Peter 4:10, Revelation 1:6). While there are certainly gifts of leadership given to some, all are part of the priesthood, having received of the Spirit. Thus, all are *in* the ministry.

It was Martin Luther during the Reformation who gave voice to this long-forgotten doctrine that all believers share a common priesthood:

> *"That the pope or bishop anoints, makes tonsures, ordains, consecrates, or dresses differently from the laity, may make a hypocrite or an idolatrous oil-painted icon, but it in no way makes a Christian or spiritual human being. In fact, we are all consecrated priests through Baptism, as St. Peter in 1 Peter 2[:9] says, "You are a royal priesthood and a priestly kingdom," and Revelation [5:10], "Through your blood you have made us into priests and kings" (Martin Luther, Weimar Ausgabe, vol. 6, p. 407, lines 19–25 as quoted in Timothy Wengert, "The Priesthood of All Believers and Other Pious Myths," page 12).*

But even though Luther articulated this doctrine of the priesthood of the believer, there still remained a distinction between the priests who actually engaged in spiritual work and the rest of the Church who were engaged in secular activity. Tradition dies hard. And judging from what we see in most churches today, that division is alive and well. Protestants may tout the idea that all of God's people are priests, but in reality, pastors function as priests for the people in many churches. And many of God's people seem fine with the fact that the pastor engages totally in spiritual work while the majority of God's people pursue their secular callings.

Of course, the New Testament reveals that God's plan from the beginning was that all of God's people would serve him as priests, having direct access to his throne. When God redeemed a people from Egypt and brought them to a mountain, he stated his intention that all of his people serve him as priests (Exodus 19:5-6). It was only afterwards, because of the judgment due their worshipping the golden calf, that God rejected the priesthood and chose the tribe of Levi instead. Since that time, Israel lived in the two-tiered reality: only one of the twelve tribes could come near the Lord or his holy things while the rest had to receive through them. But God never reneged on the idea that all of God's people would one day serve him as priests.

And that day came at Pentecost, when the Holy Spirit filled 120 believers and the priesthood was on! Each believer, filled with the glory of God, was now a functioning priest/king, serving God and other believers. While some were called to be leaders, all shared in one High Priest, the mediator between God and man, the Man Christ Jesus.

Still, most churches have a two-tier hierarchy of leaders serving and doing spiritual work, while the rest serve in supportive roles. By perpetuating this, the reality of the New Covenant is continually obscured. What is the answer? It is to embrace the New Covenant fully by first making sure that we are preaching the unsearchable riches of Christ, calling people to the true altar of his cross-work, and releasing the priesthood to function in their God-given spheres and callings. In a word, it is to call our churches to fully function under a New Covenant paradigm. This is the challenge pastors and leaders have today: to insure the churches we serve are fully living out the full blessing of New Covenant reality.

WHAT IS MOST NEEDED

What is most needed today is for the churches to not only proclaim the New Covenant but also live it in reality. Leaders must make sure that they are teaching and preaching the riches of the New Covenant. All our discipling efforts need to be rooted and grounded in the realities of the New Covenant. All relationships need to be ignited by the truth of the New Covenant. All church ministries offered must be a by-product of people responding to the New Covenant.

In a word, what is most needed today is that our churches be communities of New Covenant saints who are continually coming to know and believe the New Covenant. The result will be the emergence of communities who, through the truth of the grace of God, powerfully confront a dying world with the reality of Jesus. May God hasten the day.

EPILOGUE

Finishing a book is a difficult task. The author is tempted to look back over the work and conclude that something vital has been left out. Some books are never completed because of this. Knowing this, I now submit this work to the reader knowing that, while much more could have been said, this will suffice in communicating the message.

I know of nothing more important for the Church today than that its members understand, believe, and live out the measure of New Covenant reality. One of the saddest things on earth to see is New Covenant saints living condemned, frustrated lives, deprived of this blessing. The only answer is for the New Covenant in its fullness to be once again taught in our churches. Preachers and teachers must make it their primary aim to ensure that their hearers are well grounded in New Covenant reality.

Nowhere is this more important than when it comes to the Church's discipleship; its means of teaching and discipling new converts. Disciple makers must cease teaching principles, moralism, and must labor to unpack the full measure of the New Covenant. We simply can't afford to get this wrong when it comes to our teaching and training new generations of Christians. I know of many Church discipleship courses where converts learn various biblical principles while remaining strangers to the New Covenant, even though they graduated the course. Is it any wonder that our churches more closely resemble an Old Covenant paradigm rather than New Covenant communities where people are learning to live in freedom?

To that end, it is my prayer that God will use this book to spur a revival of New Covenant theology which will produce a harvest of transformed lives to the glory of God and the Lord Jesus Christ. Amen.

CPSIA information can be obtained
at www.ICGtesting.com
Printed in the USA
LVOW11s0503270418
575076LV00001BA/18/P